Web-Based Teaching and Learning across Culture and Age

Fengfeng Ke • Alicia Fedelina Chávez

Web-Based Teaching and Learning across Culture and Age

Springer

Fengfeng Ke
Educational Psychology
and Learning Systems
Florida State University
Tallahassee, FL, USA

Alicia Fedelina Chávez
Teacher Education, Educational
Leadership & Policy
University of New Mexico
Albuquerque, NM, USA

ISBN 978-1-4614-0862-8 ISBN 978-1-4614-0863-5 (eBook)
DOI 10.1007/978-1-4614-0863-5
Springer New York Heidelberg Dordrecht London

Library of Congress Control Number: 2013935497

Printed on acid-free paper

Springer is part of Springer Science+Business Media (www.springer.com)

Preface

The findings and discussions in this work are based on a 2-year research project funded by Spencer Foundation research grant # 200800124. The authors would like to thank all participating online instructors and students for their support and valuable input. The authors would also like to thank Felisha Herrera, Michelle Jewett, Penny L. Causarano, Dean Kwak, Tatiana Abras, Rebeca Gibrail, and all of the people who have assisted our work.

Tallahassee, FL, USA — Fengfeng Ke
Albuquerque, NM, USA — Alicia Fedelina Chávez

Contents

Part I
Diversity in Online Learning Contexts

Chapter 1
Introduction and Background

It has been suggested that the flexibility and cost-effectiveness of web-based online courses and programs should be particularly helpful in bringing a broader base of population into postsecondary education (Finkelstein, Frances, Jewett, & Scholz, 2000; Radford, Berkner, Wheeless, & Shepherd, 2011). A recent major report about online learning in US higher education (Allen & Seaman, 2010) indicated that for the past 6 years, online enrollments have grown substantially faster (i.e., 17 % growth rate) than overall higher education enrollments (1.2 % growth rate) and are demonstrating no signs of slowing. More than one in four college and university students take at least one course online. Virtually all types of collegiate institutions show substantial growth: Three-quarters of institutions reported increased demand for *new* (or *existing*) online courses and programs, and student demand for online offerings is greater than for corresponding face-to-face offerings.

Online pedagogy should differ from that in face-to-face classes. Modes of learning, interactions, opportunities, and challenges differ greatly in web-based learning contexts and should be conceptualized and developed accordingly. Growth of online courses and programs has increased the need for faculty to become comfortable with online teaching and gain the necessary design and pedagogical skills to make online courses a success. Ironically, recent reports about online education found that generally there is no systematic training focused in online pedagogy and faculty perceptions and acceptance of online teaching and learning has changed little in recent years. It is concluded that "quality still looms as a large question for online education" (WCET, 2010).

Contemporary higher education, especially web-based distance education, reflects increasing age diversity rather than the traditional student age profile – a person who is 17–22 years old. As a major grouping, adult learners over age 24 now comprise more than 44 % of current postsecondary populations in America (Radford et al., 2011). Older adult students are particularly interested in web-based distance education and participate in both online classes and degree programs more often than their counterparts (Eduventures, 2005; Radford et al., 2011). Adult learners exhibit significant differences in their academic, psychological, and life involvements from traditional students (Richardson & King, 1998; Schlossberg, Lynch, &

F. Ke and A.F. Chávez, *Web-Based Teaching and Learning across Culture and Age*,
DOI 10.1007/978-1-4614-0863-5_1, © Springer Science+Business Media New York 2013

Chickering, 1989). Most adult learners work part time or full time, have dependents, and must juggle school with the responsibilities of family, work, and community service. Adults persist and graduate at rates lower than traditional students (Kazis et al., 2007). As such, it is critical to understand the learning needs of adult learners to design successful higher education. However, practices and policies of higher education systems, such as program structure and duration, pedagogy, and learner support, continue to favor traditional, financially dependent, 18- to 21-year-old high school graduates who enroll full time (Kazis et al.).

Recently, undergraduate minority student enrollments, Hispanics/Latinos and Asians/Pacific Islanders in particular, are increasing at rates faster than Whites. Trends in graduate enrollments are similar (NCES, 2010). There are also indications that more students of color are pursuing degrees through online education. For example, of those Native American students awarded master's degrees in the last 5 years, many have obtained graduate degrees through web-based programs (Secatero, 2009). Some scholars argue that online education allows minority students to participate in education while remaining within the support of their families, cultures, and communities instead of facing the significant challenges of predominantly White campuses. Some posit that this may lead to higher levels of success and retention. On the other hand, there is concern in the literature that minority students may be disadvantaged online because of cultural incongruences in pedagogies as well as less technological access (McLoughlin & Oliver, 2000). Culture pervades learning, and technology-mediated online learning environments are encoded with the same cultural values and assumptions of their developers (Johns & Kelley Sipp, 2004). Online educational practices and environments are likely to be incongruent with students' preexisting cultural dispositions associated with ethnicity or age and influence their learning processes, needs, actions, and thoughts.

Therefore, it is critical to design web-based learning contexts effective across culture and age, by considering the potential cultural and age-related diversity in online learners' technological usage, online learning participation and satisfaction, and the performance of learning interactions with the content, online instructor, and peers.

Culture and Age Diversity in Designing Inclusive Learning Environments

Definitions of Culture

Early in 1952, Kroeber and Kluckhohn published a critical review and analysis of 200 different definitions of culture categorized into six groups: descriptive, historical, normative, psychological, structural, and genetic (Baldwin, Faulkner, Hecht, & Lindsley, 2006). A descriptive or structural definition of culture emphasizes enumeration or patterning of content in cultural activities and habits. A famous one by Tylor (1871) states, "Culture …is that complex whole which includes knowledge, belief, art, law, morals, custom, and any other capabilities and habits acquired by man as a member of society" (p. 4). Similarly, Willey (1929) defined culture as a system of interrelated and interdependent habit patterns of a social group. A common definition of culture characterizes it as the sum of rules or ways of doing and thinking within a social group. A historical definition of culture emphasizes social heritage or tradition. For example, Sapir (1921) defined culture as "the socially inherited assemblage of practices and beliefs that determines the texture of our lives" (p. 221). Psychological definitions describe culture as a dynamic process – the adjustment of humans to their surroundings and needs that are attained via variation, selection, and transmission. Along the same line, genetic definitions of culture portray it as a product or artifact created by humans when we adjust ourselves to our environment.

In summary, the conceptualization of culture comprises two primary dimensions: a set of existing patterns, habits, or rules of thinking and doing of a social group and the dynamic adjustment of this social group to surroundings and needs, which then create a sum total of rules or patterns of acting/thinking to be inherited by future members of the group. In this book, we emphasize and integrate both dimensions in our research findings, discussion, and recommendations.

Ethnicity- and Age-Related Cultural Diversities

In early research, culture was typically treated as a collective trait or activity. Hofstede (1984) defined culture as "the collective programming of the mind which distinguishes the members of one group or category of people from another" (p. 51). This definition highlights culture as a collective activity or identity that is formed via the "similarity of individuals within a cohort group (be it a linguistic community, an ethnic group or a scientific community)" (Vatrapu & Suthers, 2007, p. 262). Additionally, empirical research on cultural differences is primarily focused on nationality-based cultural patterns. For example, by extending Hall's low-context and high-context cultural factors (1976), Hofstede's cultural dimensions model (Hofstede, Hofstede, & Minkov, 2010) lists six dimensions deployed mainly to describe different nationality cultural groups: low versus high power distance, individualism versus collectivism, femininity versus masculinity, high versus low uncertainty avoidance, short-term versus long-term orientation, and indulgence versus restraint.

Less research effort and discussion contributes to ethnic- and age-related social or cultural groups, especially when two social or cultural groups are examined simultaneously. Additionally, culture should be viewed as a fragmented rather than coherent latent variable (Baldwin et al., 2006; DiMaggio, 1997; Vatrapu & Suthers, 2007). A learner group's cultural disposition will usually interact with and be fragmented by characteristics of individual members and external contextual factors (e.g., organizational culture or disciplinary effect). Individual differences among members of a social group, comprising their internal individual needs and efforts to adjust to the external environment, tend to be ignored in prior research.

Theoretical Perspectives on the Effect of Cultural and Age Differences on Cognition, Communication, and Behavior

Cultural Effect

Scholars argue that research evidence casts substantial doubt on assumptions of cognition's universality and content independence (Nisbett & Norenzayan, 2002). Based on the perspective of cognitive anthropology, culture profoundly influences content of thought. D'Andrade (1995) and Nishida (1999), in particular, extended the concept of cognitive schema to introduce the notion of cultural schemas – schemas that make up the meaning systems of a cultural group and are intersubjectively shared in the group to form cultural models. Cultural schemas and models govern the ways by which people in the social group take part in activities, use the objects, perform actions, and interpret their experiences (Nisbett & Norenzayan, 2002). The cultural schema notion helps to explain how contents of thought can differ across cultures.

Cultural groups differ in not only the contents of human minds but also the very thought processes by which people cognize the world, such as the inferential procedures typically used for a given problem and patterns of references (DiMaggio, 1997; Fellbaum & Vossen, 2007; Nisbett & Norenzayan, 2002; Ross, 2003). Based on the perspectives of sociocultural psychology and situated cognition (Cole, 1996; Heine, 2008; Vygotsky, 1978), cultural variation in cognition is a result of the different historical development of a social group, leading to different social activities and tools, which then lead to different cognitive processes (Nisbett & Norenzayan, 2002). For example, some cultural groups prefer holistic, formal reasoning while others prefer analytic, intuitive reasoning (Nisbett, Peng, Choi, & Norenzayan, 2001). According to the linguistic relativity hypothesis (Whorf, 1956), the particular language people speak or linguistic difference affects thought. Empirical evidence exists suggesting the cognitive effect of linguistic differences (Nisbett & Norenzayan, 2002).

Culture is also believed to be associated with social behavior (Hofstede, 2001; House, Hanges, Javidan, Dorfman, & Gupta, 2004; Trompenaars & Hampden-Turner, 1998) and communication (Hall, 1985). Based on Hofstede's cultural dimensions model (Hofstede et al., 2010), cultural groups may differ in the degree to which a group handles inequalities among people (i.e., power distance), a preference for a loosely knit social framework or a tightly knit framework (i.e., individualism vs. collectivism), a preference for achievement/competition or cooperation/modesty (i.e., masculinity vs. femininity), the degree to which members of a social group feel uncomfortable with uncertainty and ambiguity (i.e., uncertainty avoidance), a focus on short-term or long-term orientation, and a preference for indulgence or restraint in the gratification of needs. Hall's cultural factors (1985) describe observed cultural differences in communication, comprising the degree of reliance on contextual elements in understanding the rules or the degree of overtness of messages (i.e., high context vs. low context), the preference of human interaction over time and material things (polychromic time vs. monochromic time), and the need for personal space and ownership of territoriality.

It should be noted that culture is not always coherent around social groupings but can be heterogeneous in content and function (DiMaggio, 1997). Prior research (e.g., Gilbert, 1991; Parrish & Linder-Vanberschot, 2010; Vatrapu, 2008) indicates that individuals are capable of participating in multiple cultural traditions that contain inconsistent elements and maintaining multiple cultural frames while adopting a host culture in response to particular contextual cues. Moreover, Vatrapu and Suthers (2007) argued that cultural schemas are formed dynamically from an individual's biography that "includes the interactive effects of the geography of that individual's upbringing (ecology) and the formative experiences of his/her life (history)" (p. 262). In other terms, there is potentially an interactive effect between the culture of a social group and the background, experience, and acculturation competency of individuals in the social group on their cognition, communication, and behavior in social events.

Effect of Age

Research in cognitive aging reveals that *crystallized intelligence*, such as general world knowledge, specified knowledge in areas of expertise, and verbal abilities closely related to reading, are mostly stable and may even show improvement across the adult life-span (Hess & Hinson, 2006; Meyer & Pollard, 2006; Schaie, 2005). Performance on tasks tapping expertise in these crystallized abilities or tasks that require solving interpersonal problems generally maintains, if not increases, across adulthood (Carstensen, Mikels, & Mather, 2006). On the other hand, performance on tasks that require effortful and resource-intensive processing (or *fluid intelligence*), such as speed of processing, executive function, working memory, recall long-term memory, selective attention, divided attention, or fluent language production, tends to decline with age (Burke & Shafto, 2004; Hess & Hinson, 2006; Hoyer & Verhaeghen, 2006; Miyake, Carpenter, & Just, 1995; Park et al., 2002; Thornton & Light, 2006).

There is also interaction between emotion and cognition across the adult life-span based on the socioemotional aging research (Carstensen, Isaacowitz, & Charles, 1999; Carstensen et al., 2006). Later in life when time is typically perceived as constrained, individuals will heighten attention to the regulation of emotion states and allocate more cognitive resources to emotional tasks, which results in selective cognitive processing. For example, a growing body of research suggests that older adults are likely to devote cognitive resources to information that will enhance their emotional mood, whereas younger people tend to favor negative materials in information processing (Carstensen & Mikels, 2005).

On the other hand, the literature generally asserts that age-related changes differ across individuals. Besides genetic, health-related factors, individual lifestyles (e.g., education level, activities engaged) and motivation factors (e.g., attitudes toward a specific topic) will mediate cognitive functioning across age groups.

Theoretical Perspectives on Cultural and Age Differences in Technology-Mediated Operations

There is growing evidence of the cultural effect on technology-mediated operations. Human-computer interaction (HCI) research indicates that culture influences *user interface design* (e.g., Bourges-Waldegg & Scrivener, 1998; Del Gado & Nielsen, 1996; Khaslavsky, 1998), *usability processes and evaluation* (e.g., Vatrapu & Suthers, 2007; Yammiyavar, Clemmensen, & Kumar, 2008), and *web design* (e.g., Faiola & Matei, 2006; Marcus & Gould, 2000; Matei & Ball-Rokeach, 2001; Sears, Jacko, & Dubach, 2000). Prior research also indicated cultural effects on *computer-mediated communication (CMC)* (e.g., Danet & Herring, 2007; Ess & Sudweeks, 2005; Herring, 1996) and *computer-supported collaborative work or learning (CSCW* or *CSCL)* (e.g., Setlock & Fussell, 2010; Vatrapu & Suthers, 2007; Wang, Fussell, & Setlock, 2009).

Technology can act as a mediating factor between learners and learning. According to Vatrapu (2008, 2009), technology-mediated learning environments are characterized by socio-technical interactions (conceived as the *social-technical affordances* of the learning environment) in which individuals interact with technologies and with other individuals via technologies (called *technological intersubjectivity*). Social affordances of technology-mediated learning environments might vary along cultural dimensions of learners (Vatrapu, 2008). First, technology may make interactions more difficult for certain cultural dimensions. Second, technology-mediated interactions may mean, feel, or afford different things across cultural cognitive and communication styles (Faiola & Matei, 2006). Members of different cultures appropriate resources differently in their interactions and form differential relations with and impressions of each other (Vatrapu, 2008).

It can be more difficult for older individuals to process computer-generated information and use communications technology to share or search information, due to age-related changes in vision, working memory, and attention-switching capability (Scialfa, Ho, & Laberge, 2004). Prior research also suggests that older individuals' technology usage is influenced more by subjective norms and perceived behavioral control, while younger individuals' technology usage is influenced more by attitudes toward using technology (Morris & Venkatesh, 2000). Still, the effect of aging on the adoption and usage of technology-mediated interactions is not coherent. Study findings indicate that using technology can be highly stratified by gender and educational background among older adults (Selwyn, Gorard, Furlong, & Madden, 2003).

Web-Based Education Across Culture and Age

A recent review of the literature (Ke, Jewett, & Chávez, 2010) suggests, scholars generally argue that technology-mediated online learning environments are infused with cultural values. Certain cultural groups (e.g., minority or older adult students) can be disadvantaged online. Yet few arguments about web-based education across culture and age are based on empirical studies or provide solid data on cultural and age-related diversities in people's online learning process and success.

Prior efforts in describing an *inclusive* (i.e., multicultural and intergenerational) instructional design model for online learning were frequently based on theoretical propositions or anecdotal notes and observations of a single online course or program. A common suggestion by scholars on the "inclusive" design of online learning environment is to provide a "balance" of nationality-, ethnicity-, or age-related cultural dimensions via the design and selection of technology, content, activity, and facilitation strategies that are culturally inclusive, thus creating an *eclectic paradigm* that incorporates multiple cultural perspectives (Anderson & Simpson, 2007; Henderson, 1996, 1997; Rasmussen, Nichols, & Ferguson, 2006). But it is ambiguous as to how such a balanced inclusion or integration is achieved during the online learning and instruction process, or what an eclectic, culturally inclusive online learning environment is like. Scholars, taking an evaluative and interpretive approach, have focused on analyzing and describing cultural variation and commonness in an effort to explore the nature of culturally inclusive learning tools or contexts (e.g., Adeoye & Wentling, 2007; Anakwe, Kessler, & Christensen, 1999; Dillon, Wang, & Tearle, 2007; Hudson, Hudson & Steel, 2006; Hurd & Xiao, 2006; Lim, 2004; Selinger, 2004; Wang, 2007). For example, Vatrapu and Suthers (2010) proposed a purposeful analysis of the cultural usability of emerging technology by examining the cultural variation at the level of human-computer interaction, thus informing the design of the techno-social affordance (i.e., action-taking and meaning-making opportunities) of the technology for diverse nationality-related cultural groups.

An alternative to the "balance" proposition is the argument for "flexibility" in "adapting" course dimensions to a target cultural or age group (Collis, Vingerhoets, & Moonen, 1997; Hogan, 2009; Ibarra, 2000; Knight, Dixon, Norton, & Bentley, 2004; Lin, 2007; Llambi et al., 2008; Sanchez, Stuckey, & Morris, 1998; Sang, 2007; Zepke & Leach, 2002). Constructivism-oriented instructional strategies are predominantly mentioned and discussed as the representation of culturally responsive solutions to a minority or older adult learner group (e.g., Gunawardena, Wilson, & Nolla, 2003; Smith & Ayers, 2006; McLoughlin & Oliver, 2000). Specifically, collaborative learning (e.g., community of inquiry), active learning, inductive and application-based knowledge building, and dynamic technology requirements have been proposed. Yet systematic investigations on these propositions with empirical evidence are still lacking.

Scholars such as Dillon et al. (2007) and Gunawardena et al. (2003) reason that cultural connection or disconnection is an interaction between outer culture characteristics (e.g., national or ethnicity-related culture), inner culture characteristics (e.g., individual personality, learning style, technological competency, gender, and personal expectation), and the academic culture of the educational environment (e.g., time frame/structure/protocol of virtual grouping). Such a cultural connection or disconnection may be reflected in learning strategies used, online participation/interaction performance, and hence an individual's satisfaction/confidence about learning online. However, prior research on web-based education across culture and age generally focused on examining the interaction between outer culture characteristics (e.g., the high- versus low-context cultural dimension) of cultural group(s) and the academic culture in the educational environment, with few conceiving of the inner culture characteristics of individuals in the group.

Research on Cultural Issues in Web-Based Education

There is limited research to date about the impact of various teaching techniques on diverse cultural groups within the online classroom and minimum extant research on the connection between cultural dimensions and the design of effective online education (Wang & Reeves, 2007). According to Goodfellow and Hewling (2005), cultural issues in an online learning environment can be summarized as related to three major themes: the development of inequities arising from *dominant* cultural values embodied in teaching materials and methods (e.g., Gunawardena et al., 2003); the potential miscommunication among participants during online discussions or other collaborative learning activities, arising from cultural difference (e.g., Wong & Trinidad, 2004); and the emergence of learning or academic culture (e.g., sense of community and inquiry culture) within an online course or program(e.g., Hakkarainen, 2003). Aligning with such a framework, in this book, *culture* includes (1) dispositions, learning and communication styles brought by individual students (with their preexisting cultural characteristics) to an online learning environment, and (2) patterns of participation engaged by online students, which hence creates a special learning or academic culture within an online learning environment.

Prior research on traditional learning environments generally suggests that learners and instructors struggle when there is a collision of different cultures. Web-based learning environments, in comparison with traditional learning environments, are not immune to the problems arising from cultural differences (Uzuner, 2009). In fact, they may be more prone to cultural conflicts because technology can introduce a novel learning and instruction culture that is at odds with typical learning or instructional thoughts and actions.

Based on previous studies, potential cultural issues in an online learning environment may arise due to language differences in online content and communication (Joo, 1999), an inherent conflict between the individualism, low-context norm of online pedagogies and collectivism, high-context norm of many students' cultural values (Adeoye & Wentling, 2007; Anakwe et al. 1999; Ibarra, 2000; Tu, 2001; Wang, 2007), differences in student beliefs about the value and nature of knowledge and how one acquires knowledge (Chen, Bennett, & Maton, 2008; Makoe, 2006), or other culture-related learning or reasoning style differentials (Bentley, Tinney, & Chia, 2005).

Although previous studies generally proclaim the need to ensure cultural responsiveness or accommodation, it is difficult for an instructor or designer to accommodate each and every culture of learners. Problems arise when the core pedagogical values in one culture are culturally inappropriate in another (Reeves & Reeves, 1997). Still, generic heuristics and principles were proposed for constructing and implementing culturally relevant online pedagogy or culturally sensitive online learning environments (e.g., Bentley et al., 2005; Collis, 1999; McLoughlin & Oliver, 2000; Wang & Reeves, 2007). Two of the most frequently proposed principles are (1) creating constructivist online environments that are explicit and equitable and (2) allowing different, alternating configurations of pedagogical dimensions (e.g., the modes of online communication; the nature of learning tasks, academic and authentic; the role of the instructor, didactic and facilitative; & the availability and presentation of course materials).

Prior research on technology-mediated learning for cross-cultural learners also contributes useful frameworks for understanding and dealing with issues of culture in online education. For example, Henderson (1996) presented a Multiple Cultural Pedagogic Model of interactive multimedia instructional design based in turn on the 14 dimensions of interactive learning of Reeves (1997). These cultural dimensions include group size and task type, pedagogic philosophy (e.g., instructivist or constructivist, deep or surface learning, horizontal or vertical communication), language and visual aspects of the user interface, technology-related infrastructure differences, expected roles/responsibilities of learners/instructors, human-computer interaction, and institutional culture and policy. Similarly, Collis et al. (1997) summarized 19 dimensions which could be either fixed or flexible in a course using advanced learning technologies. The dimensions included four related to time (time of starting and finishing a course, time expectations within a course, tempo of studying, and timing of assessments), five related to content of the course (flexibility related to the topics covered, sequence in which topics are covered, amount and scope of content, level, and assessment criteria), one related to flexibility in expected prerequisites, four related to instructional approach and resources (social or individual learning activities, language used, study materials, and pedagogic approach), and five related to course delivery and logistics (time and place where help can be obtained, way of obtaining help, types of help, locations for participating in the course, and delivery channels including face-to-face and technology-mediated varieties). Parrish and Linder-VanBerschot (2010), by synthesizing prior research on nationality-related cultural dimensions (Hall, 1983; Hofstede, Hofstede, & Minkov, 2010; Levine, 1997; Lewis, 2006; Nisbett, 2003), presented a Cultural Dimensions of Learning Framework that outlined spectrums of cultural diversities and acted as a cultural analysis and refection tool for online instruction providers. The aforementioned theoretical or design frameworks for culture in technology-based education, in general, lack empirical investigation, evaluation, and data support. To a certain degree, theory development has outpaced development in practice.

Research on Age-Related Diversity in Online Education

Student status related to age is not as commonly investigated as ethnicity- or nationality-related culture when it comes to online education research. In spite of powerful initiatives promulgating opportunities for wider access to higher education, there is little empirical evidence of a more comprehensive and open system for nontraditional students (Ke & Carr-Chellman, 2006). Research on web-based learning environments, like that for traditional learning settings, has generally focused on the learning success of traditional college students.

Frequently web-based online education students are adults over age 24 and nontraditional students. The definition of adult or nontraditional students varies in prior research. Most often adult or nontraditional students are defined as ones who returned to or reentered their postsecondary education at age 24 or older or are enrolling on less than a full-time basis (Davis, 2006; Richardson & King, 1998; McGivney, 2004). These students exhibit significant differences in academic, psychological, and life involvements from traditional students (Guido-DiBrito & Chávez, 2003; Richardson & King, 1998).

A common speculation in the literature about online higher education is that older adult students tend to find online learning difficult to adapt to and demand more support services and technology training. On the other hand, online education offers flexibility of time and space and hence suits adult students who have to arrange their classes around work and family responsibilities and will experience more constraints in time and scheduling (Cercone, 2008). There is empirical evidence suggesting online learning processes and outcomes may differ by age (Justice & Dornan, 2001). For example, the studies by Chyung (2007) and Hoskins and van Hooff (2005) indicated that older adult students posted significantly more online messages, but younger students improved their self-efficacy toward learning topics significantly more. Wyatt (2005) reported in his survey research that age was positively associated with the perception that online instruction provided a quality experience. Older students were found to be more likely to have a *converger* learning style, learning best through active experimentation and abstract conceptualization (e.g., forming theories from observations and reflections) (Buerck, Malmstrom, & Peppers, 2003). In addition, successful online adult learners often demonstrated a higher self-directed learning ability and IT skills (Shinkareva & Benson, 2007).

Studies on online education for adult or nontraditional students are sparse. A recent search in national databases ERIC and Educational Research Complete of the terms "nontraditional" or "adult student" and "distance education" (and variations of these terms) resulted in the identification of only 13 articles. The limited articles on intergenerational instruction provide mainly anecdotal and heuristic advices. Specifically, authors recommend flexibility with deadlines, more time, smaller units, real-world activities, and a community-like online learning environment (Davis, 2006; McGivney, 2004; Patton, 2000; Sorensen & Murchú, 2004). The diversity of adults in terms of age, educational attainment, and socioeconomic and personal circumstances often results in patterns of learning engagement considerably different from those of younger students (McGivney 2004). Corresponding to nontraditional and adult students' learning profiles, certain generic instructional design principles have also been speculated. Recently, Cercone (2008), Githens (2007), and Majeski and Stover (2007) prescribed a series of heuristic design principles for online adult learning. These principles shared the same key characteristics as those of high-quality online pedagogies or strategies for general learners, such as collaboration with peers, experience- and application-based learning, a climate of self-reflection, and self-regulated learning.

Although prior research, mostly theoretical speculations, laid out a potential framework on adult-serving online course design, they were supported by only anecdotal evidence and there appears to be limited research available to support this evidence. Few in situ studies were conducted to examine the nature of intergenerational education in an online setting or how web-based learning environments and pedagogies can be created and implemented to serve intergenerational learners equitably.

Summary

Prior research indicates that cultural and age-related diversity mediates individuals' cognition, communication, behavior, technology-mediated interaction, and hence web-based online learning. Yet systematic and empirical investigations on web-based teaching and learning for multicultural and intergenerational students are sparse. Descriptions of the interaction between students' cultural diversity, online learning environments, and students' learning and participation behaviors are still primarily anecdotal. Suggestions on the design and implementation of multicultural and intergenerational online learning are typically generic and murky.

An Outline of the Book

During academic years 2008–2010, we conducted a 2-year, mixed-method study to explore the impact of online pedagogies and contexts on the learning processes and perceptions of a diversity of college students living in rural and urban areas, with an emphasis on learners of nontraditional age and minority status. For this longitudinal study, we collected data from 36 WebCT-based online courses across 12 academic disciplines at a major research university in the southwestern United States. The study contributes a variety of findings on the dynamic role of online learners' culture- and age-related identities in their learning participation and interaction performance. Study data and findings serve as a basis for the development of an analysis framework of critical cultural constructs in the online learning setting and an *inclusive* design framework for cross-cultural and intergenerational online learning.

Based on the study, this book presents data-driven findings and discussions on web-based multicultural and intergenerational learning as well as recommendations for teaching practice and future research. The book is comprised of three parts. Part 1 provides an introduction to the motivation, theoretical framework, and major methodologies of the study. Chapter 1 defines and describes culture- and age-related diversity and its role in cognition, communication, technology-mediated interaction, and hence online learning. Chapter 2 provides an elaborative review and discussion of prior research with findings and theoretical lenses on multicultural and intergenerational teaching and learning. In Chapter 3, we provide an overview of the 2-year, mixed-method study, with a focus on the research design and data collection/analysis methods.

Part 2 presents salient study findings. Chapter 4 synthesizes data illustrating the presence and potential effects of online learners' cultural- and age-related diversity on their online learning interaction performance, learning satisfaction, and perceived learner success. Chapter 5 describes and discusses a design and analysis model of eight cultural constructs in teaching and learning derived from student narrative data. Chapter 6 presents data-driven, verified structural equation models on interactions between individual characteristics, cultural and age status, instructional contexts, online learning strategies, and online learning success.

In Part 3, we discuss and propose an instructional design framework for multicultural and intergenerational online learning success. Specifically, in Chapter 7, we discuss implications of the study findings and the potential of developing a participatory, fluid design process for content, interface, activity, and technological infrastructure design. Chapter 8 highlights salient online instructional contextual features that promote inclusive, deep learning for learners of different ethnic and age groups. Chapter 9, the final chapter, synthesizes all relative findings to discuss potential and future research on developing a balanced and inclusive instructional design model for multicultural and intergenerational online teaching and learning as well as some wider considerations in colleges and universities.

References

Adeoye, B., & Wentling, R. (2007). The relationship between national culture and the usability of an e-learning system. *International Journal on E-Learning, 6*(1), 119–146.

Allen, I. E., & Seaman, J. (2010). *Class differences: Online education in the United States, 2010.* Retrieved November 8, 2011 from http://sloanconsortium.org/sites/default/files/class_differences.pdf.

Anakwe, U. P., Kessler, E. H., & Christensen, E. W. (1999). Distance learning and cultural diversity: Potential users' perspective. *International Journal of Organizational Analysis, 7*(3), 224–243.

Anderson, B., & Simpson, M. (2007). Ethical issues in online education. *Open Learning, 22*(2), 129–138. Retrieved March 29, 2009, doi:10.1080/02680510701306673.

Baldwin, J. R., Faulkner, S. L., Hecht, M. L., & Lindsley, S. L. (Eds.). (2006). *Redefining culture: Perspectives across the disciplines.* Mahwah: Lawrence Erlbaum.

Bentley, J. P. H., Tinney, M. V., & Chia, B. H. (2005). Intercultural internet-based learning: Know your audience and what it values. *Educational Technology Research and Development, 53*(2), 117–127.

Bourges-Waldegg, P., & Scrivener, S. A. (1998). Meaning, the central issue in cross-cultural HCI design. *Interacting with Computers, 9*(3), 287–309.

Buerck, J., Malmstrom, T., & Peppers, E. (2003). Learning environments and learning styles: Non-traditional student enrollment and success in an internet-based versus a lecture-based computer science course. *Learning Environments Research, 6*(2), 137–155.

Burke, D. M., & Shafto, M. A. (2004). Aging and language production. *Current Directions in Psychological Science, 13*(1), 21–24.

Carstensen, L. L., Isaacowitz, D. M., & Charles, S. T. (1999). Taking time seriously: A theory of socioemotional selectivity. *American Psychologist, 54*(3), 165–181.
Carstensen, L. L., & Mikels, J. A. (2005). At the intersection of emotion and cognition: Aging and the positivity effect. *Current Directions in Psychological Science, 14*(3), 117–121.
Carstensen, L. L., Mikels, J. A., & Mather, M. (2006). Aging and the intersection of cognition, motivation, and emotion. In J. Birren & K. W. Schaie (Eds.), *Handbook of the psychology of aging* (pp. 343–362). San Diego, CA: Elsevier.
Cercone, K. (2008). Characteristics of adult learners with implications for online learning design. *AACE Journal, 16*(2), 137–159.
Chen, R. T., Bennett, S., & Maton, K. (2008). The adaptation of Chinese international students to online flexible learning: two case studies. *Distance Education, 29*(3), 307–323. Retrieved March 29, 2009, doi:10.1080/01587910802395821
Chyung, S. (2007). Age and gender differences in online behavior, self-efficacy, and academic performance. *Quarterly Review of Distance Education, 8*(3), 213–222. Retrieved March 29, 2009, from Education Research Complete database.
Cole, M. (1996). *Cultural psychology: A once and future discipline*. Cambridge: Belknap Press of Harvard University Press.
Collis, B. (1999). Designing for differences: Cultural issues in the design of WWW-based course-support sites. *British Journal of Educational Technology, 30*(3), 201–215.
Collis, B., Moonen, J., & Vingerhoets, J. (1997). Flexibility as a key construct in European training: Experiences from the TeleScopia project. *British Journal of Educational Technology, 28*(3), 199–217.
d'Andrade, R. G. (1995). *The development of cognitive anthropology*. Cambridge: Cambridge University Press.
Danet, B., & Herring, S. C. (Eds.). (2007). *The multilingual internet: Language, culture, and communication online*. Oxford: Oxford University Press.
Davis, J. (2006). Designing an online course for nontraditional students: Revisiting the essentials. *International Journal of Learning, 12*(10), 121–127.
Del Gado, E., & Nielsen, J. (Eds.). (1996). *International user interfaces*. New York: Wiley.
Dillon, P., Wang, R., & Tearle, P. (2007). Cultural disconnection in virtual education. *Pedagogy, Culture & Society, 15*(2), 153–174. Retrieved March 29, 2009, doi:10.1080/14681360701403565.
DiMaggio, P. (1997). Culture and cognition. *Annual Review of Sociology, 23*, 263–287.
Eduventures. (2005). *Online distance education market update 2005: Growth in the age of competition*. Boston: Eduventures, LLC.
Ess, C., & Sudweeks, F. (2005). Culture and computer-mediated communication: Toward new understandings. *Journal of Computer-Mediated Communication, 11*(1), 179–191.
Faiola, A., & Matei, S. A. (2006). Cultural cognitive style and web design: Beyond a behavioral inquiry into computer-mediated communication. *Journal of Computer-Mediated Communication, 11*(1), 375–394.
Fellbaum, C., & Vossen, P. (2007). Connecting the universal to the specific: Towards the global grid. *Intercultural Collaboration, 4568*, 1–16.
Finkelstein, M. J., Frances, C., Jewett, F. I., & Scholz, B. W. (2000). *Dollars, distance, and online education: The new economics of college teaching and learning*. Phoenix: Oryx Press.
Gilbert, D. (1991). How mental systems believe. *American Psychologist, 46*(2), 107–119.
Githens, R. P. (2007). Older adults and e-learning: Opportunities and barriers. *The Quarterly Review of Distance Education, 8*(4), 329–338.
Goodfellow, R., & Hewling, A. (2005). Reconceptualising culture in virtual learning environments: From an 'essentialist' to a 'negotiated' perspective. *E-learning, 2*(4), 355–367.
Guido-DiBrito, F., & Chávez, A. F. (2003). Understanding the ethnic self: Learning and teaching in a multicultural world. *Journal of Student Affairs, 7*, 11–21.
Gunawardena, C., Wilson, P., & Nolla, A. (2003). Culture and online education. In M. Morre & W. Anderson (Eds.), *Handbook of distance education* (pp. 753–775). Mahwah: Lawrence Erlbaum.
Hakkarainen, K. (2003). Emergence of progressive-inquiry culture in computer-supported collaborative learning. *Learning Environment Research, 6*(2), 199–220.

Hall, E. T. (1976). *Beyond culture*. New York: Anchor Books.
Hall, E. T. (1983). *The dance of life*. New York: Doubleday.
Hall, E. T. (1985). *Hidden differences: Studies in international communication*. Hamburg: Grunder and Jahr.
Heine, S. J. (2008). *Cultural psychology*. New York: Norton.
Henderson, L. (1996). Instructional design of interactive multimedia. *Educational Technology Research and Development, 44*(4), 85–104.
Herring, S. C. (Ed.). (1996). *Computer-mediated communication: Linguistic, social, and cross-cultural perspectives*. Amsterdam: John Benjamins Publishing Co.
Hess, T. M., & Hinson, J. T. (2006). Age-related variation in the influences of aging stereotypes on memory in adulthood. *Psychology and Aging; Psychology and Aging, 21*(3), 621.
Hofstede, G. (1984). National cultures and corporate cultures. In L. A. Samovar & R. E. Porter (Eds.), *Communication between cultures*. Belmont: Wadsworth.
Hofstede, G. (2001). *Culture's consequences: Comparing values, behaviors, institutions, and organizations across nations*. Thousand Oaks: Sage.
Hofstede, G., Hofstede, G. J., & Minkov, M. (2010). *Cultures and organizations: Software of the mind, revised and expanded* (3rd ed.). New York: McGraw-Hill.
Hogan, R. (2009). Attitudes of indigenous peoples toward distance learning in the South Pacific: An empirical study. In G. Siemens & C. Fulford (Eds.), *Proceedings of world conference on educational multimedia, hypermedia and telecommunications 2009* (pp. 1064–1072). Chesapeake: AACE.
Hoskins, S. L., & Van Hooff, J. C. (2005). Motivation and ability: Which students use online learning and what influence does it have on their achievement? *British Journal of Educational Technology, 36*(2), 177–192.
House, R. J., Hanges, P. J., Javidan, M., Dorfman, P. W., & Gupta, V. (2004). *Culture, leadership, and organizations: The GLOBE study of 62 societies*. Thousand Oaks: Sage.
Hoyer, W. J., & Verhaeghen, P. (2006). Memory aging. In J. Birren & K. W. Schaie (Eds.), *Handbook of the psychology of aging* (pp. 209–232). San Diego, CA: Elsevier.
Hudson, B., Hudson, A., & Steel, J. (2006). Orchestrating interdependence in an international online learning community. *British Journal of Educational Technology, 37*(5), 733–748. Retrieved April 29, 2009, doi:10.1111/j.1467-8535.2006.00552.x.
Hurd, S., & Xiao, J. (2006). Open and distance language learning at the Shantou Radio and TV University, China, and the Open University, United Kingdom: A cross cultural perspective. *Open Learning, 21*(3), 205–219.
Ibarra, R. (2000). Studying Latinos in a "Virtual" University: Reframing diversity and academic culture change. Occasional Paper No. 68. Latino studies series. East Lansing: Julian Samora Research Institute. Retrieved March 31, 2009, from ERIC database.
Johns, A. M., & Kelley Sipp, M. (2004). *Diversity in college classrooms: Practices for today's campuses*. Ann Arbor: University of Michigan Press.
Joo, J. E. (1999). Cultural issues of the internet in classrooms. *British Journal of Educational Technology, 30*(3), 245–250.
Justice, E. M., & Dornan, T. M. (2001). Metacognitive differences between traditional-age and nontraditional-age college students. *Adult Education Quarterly, 51*(3), 236–249.
Kazis, R., Callahan, A., Davidson, C., McLeod, A., Bosworth, B., Choitz, V., et al. (2007). *Adult learners in higher education: Barriers to success and strategies to improve results*. Boston: Jobs for the Future.
Ke, F., & Carr-Chellman, A. (2006). Solitary learner in online collaborative learning: A disappointing experience? *Quarterly Review of Distance Education, 7*(3), 249–265.
Ke, F., Jewett, M., & Chávez, A. F. (2010). *Cross-cultural online education: A systematic review*. Presentation at the 2010 annual meeting of American Educational Research Association, American Educational Research Association, Denver.
Khaslavsky, J. (1998). Integrating culture into interface design. In *CHI 98 conference summary on Human factors in computing systems* (pp. 365–366). ACM.

Knight, M., Dixon, I., Norton, N., & Bentley, C. (2004). Extending learning communities: New, multiple literacies, and culture blind pedagogies. *Urban Review, 36*(2), 101–118. Retrieved March 29, 2009, from Education Research Complete database.

Kroeber, A. L., & Kluckhohn, C. (1952). *Culture: A critical review of concepts and definitions* (Papers. Peabody Museum of Archaeology & Ethnology, Harvard University). Cambridge, MA: The Museum.

Levine, R. (1997). *A geography of time*. New York: Basic Books.

Lewis, R. D. (2006). *When cultures collide: Leading across cultures* (3rd ed.). Boston: Nicholas Brealey International.

Lim, D. (2004). Cross cultural differences in online learning motivation. *Educational Media International, 41*(2), 163–173. Retrieved April 29, 2009, doi:10.1080/09523980410001685784.

Lin, C. (2007). e-Learning strategies for aboriginal children in Taiwan. *International Journal of Learning, 14*(6), 153–160. Retrieved April 29, 2009, from Education Research Complete database.

Llambi, L., Margolis, A., Toews, J., Dapueto, J., Esteves, E., Martínez, E., et al. (2008). Distance education for physicians: Adaptation of a Canadian experience to Uruguay. *Journal of Continuing Education in the Health Professions, 28*(2), 79–85. Retrieved April 29, 2009, doi:10.1002/chp.161.

Majeski, R., & Stover, M. (2007). Theoretically based pedagogical strategies leading to deep learning in asynchronous online gerontology courses. *Educational Gerontology, 33*(3), 171–185.

Makoe, M. (2006). South African distance students' accounts of learning in socio cultural context: A habitus analysis. *Race, Ethnicity & Education, 9*(4), 361–380.

Marcus, A., & Gould, E. W. (2000). Crosscurrents: Cultural dimensions and global web user-interface design. *Interactions, 7*(4), 32–46.

Matei, S., & Ball-Rokeach, S. J. (2001). Real and virtual social ties connections in the everyday lives of seven ethnic neighborhoods. *American Behavioral Scientist, 45*(3), 550–564.

McGivney, V. (2004). Understanding persistence in adult learning. *Open Learning, 19*(1), 33–46.

McLoughlin, C., & Oliver, R. (2000). Designing learning environments for cultural inclusivity: A case study of Native American online learning at tertiary level. *Australian Journal of Educational Technology, 16*(1), 58–72.

Meyer, B. J., & Pollard, C. K. (2006). Applied learning and aging: A closer look at reading. In J. Birren & K. W. Schaie (Eds.), *Handbook of the psychology of aging* (pp. 233–261). San Diego, CA: Elsevier.

Miyake, A., Carpenter, P. A., & Just, M. A. (1995). Reduced resources and specific impairments in normal and aphasic sentence comprehension. *Cognitive Neuropsychology, 12*(6), 651–679.

Morris, M. G., & Venkatesh, V. (2000). Age differences in technology adoption decisions: Implications for a changing work force. *Personnel Psychology, 53*(2), 375–403.

National Center for Educational Statistics (NCES). (2010). *Status and Trends in the Education of Racial and Ethnic Groups*. Retrieved June 10, 2012 from http://nces.ed.gov/pubs2010/2010015/index.asp.

Nisbett, R. E. (2003). *The geography of thought: How Asians and westerners think differently… And why*. New York: Free Press.

Nisbett, R. E., & Norenzayan, A. (2002). Culture and cognition. In D. L. Medin (Ed.), *Stevens' handbook of experimental psychology: Cognition* (3rd ed., pp. 561–597). New York: Wiley.

Nisbett, R. E., Peng, K., Choi, I., & Norenzayan, A. (2001). Culture and systems of thought: Holistic versus analytic cognition. *Psychological Review, 108*(2), 291–310.

Nishida, H. (1999). Cultural schema theory. In W. B. Gudykunst (Ed.), *Theorizing about intercultural communication* (pp. 401–418). Thousand Oaks, CA: Sage.

Park, D. C., Lautenschlager, G., Hedden, T., Davidson, N. S., Smith, A. D., & Smith, P. K. (2002). Models of visuospatial and verbal memory across the adult life span. *Psychology and Aging, 17*(2), 299–320.

Parrish, P., & Linder-VanBerschot, J. A. (2010). Cultural dimensions of learning: Addressing the challenges of multicultural instruction. *International Review of Research in Open and Distance Learning, 11*(2), 1–19.

Patton, M. (2000). The importance of being flexible with assignment deadlines. *Higher Education in Europe, 25*(3), 417–423.

Radford, A. W., Berkner, L., Wheeless, S. C., & Shepherd, B. (2011). *Persistence and attainment of 2003–04 beginning postsecondary students: After 6 years, NCES 2011–151*. Washington, DC: U.S. Department of Education.
Rasmussen, K., Nichols, J., & Ferguson, F. (2006). It's a new world: Multiculturalism in a virtual environment. *Distance Education, 27*(2), 265–278. Retrieved March 29, 2009, doi:10.1080/01587910600789696.
Reeves, T., & Reeves, P. (1997). Effective dimensions of interactive learning on the world wide web. In B. Khan (Ed.), *Web-based instruction* (pp. 59–66). Englewood Cliffs: Educational Technology Publications.
Richardson, J. T. E., & King, E. (1998). Adult students in higher education: Burden or boon? *Journal of Higher Education, 69*(1), 65–88.
Ross, N. (2003). *Culture and cognition: Implications for theory and method*. Thousand Oaks, CA: Sage.
Sanchez, J., Stuckey, M. E., & Morris, R. (1998). Distance learning in Indian country: Becoming the spider on the web. *Journal of American Indian Education, 37*(3), 1–17.
Sang, W. (2007). Cross-cultural delivery of e-learning programmes: Perspectives from Hong Kong. *International Review of Research in Open & Distance Learning, 8*(3), 1–16.
Sapir, E. (1921). *Language: An introduction to the study of speech* (pp. 207–220). New York: Harcourt Brace & Company.
Schaie, K. W. (2005). *Developmental influences on adult intelligence: The Seattle longitudinal study*. New York: Oxford University Press.
Schlossberg, N. K., Lynch, A. Q., & Chickering, A. W. (1989). *Improving higher education environments for adults: Responsive programs and services from entry to departure*. San Francisco: Jossey-Bass.
Scialfa, C., Ho, G., & Laberge, J. (2004). Perceptual aspects of gerotechnology. In D. C. Burdick & S. Kwon (Eds.), *Gerotechnology: Research and practice in technology and aging* (pp. 18–41). New York: Springer.
Sears, A., Jacko, J. A., & Dubach, E. M. (2000). International aspects of world wide web usability and the role of high-end graphical enhancements. *International Journal of Human Computer Interaction, 12*(2), 241–261.
Secatero, S. (2009). *Beneath our sacred minds, hands and hearts: Stories of persistence and success among American Indian graduate and professional Students*. Unpublished dissertation. University of New Mexico.
Selinger, M. (2004). Cultural and pedagogical implications of a global e-learning programme. *Cambridge Journal of Education, 34*(2), 223–239.
Selwyn, N., Gorard, S., Furlong, J., & Madden, L. (2003). Older adults' use of information and communications technology in everyday life. *Ageing and Society, 23*(5), 561–582.
Setlock, L. D., & Fussell, S. R. (2010). What's it worth to you? The costs and affordances of CMC tools to Asian and American users. In *Proceedings of the 2010 ACM conference on computer supported cooperative work* (pp. 341–350). ACM.
Shinkareva, O., & Benson, A. (2007). The relationship between adult students' instructional technology competency and self-directed learning ability in an online course. *Human Resource Development International, 10*(4), 417–435.
Smith, D., & Ayers, D. (2006). Culturally responsive pedagogy and online learning: Implications for the globalized community college. *Community College Journal of Research & Practice, 30*(5/6), 401–415.
Sorensen, E., & Murchú, D. (2004). Designing online learning communities of practice: A democratic perspective. *Journal of Educational Media, 29*(3), 189–200.
Thornton, R., & Light, L. L. (2006). Language comprehension and production in normal aging. In J. Birren & K. W. Schaie (Eds.), *Handbook of the psychology of aging* (pp. 261–287). San Diego, CA: Elsevier.
Trompenaars, F., & Hampden-Turner, C. (1998). *Riding the waves of culture*. New York: McGraw-Hill.

Tu, C. (2001). How Chinese perceive social presence: An examination of interaction in online learning environment. *Educational Media International, 38*(1), 45–60.
Tylor, E. B. (1958). *Primitive culture (1871)*. New York: JP Putnam's.
Uzuner, S. (2009). Questions of culture in distance learning: A research review. *The International Review of Research in Open and Distance Learning, 10*(3), 1–19. Retrieved January 1, 2012, from http://hdl.handle.net/10515/sy5gx4572.
Vatrapu, R. K. (2008). Cultural considerations in computer supported collaborative learning. *Research and Practice in Technology Enhanced Learning, 3*(02), 159–201.
Vatrapu, R. (2009). Towards a theory of socio-technical interactions. *Learning in the Synergy of Multiple Disciplines, 5794*, 694–699.
Vatrapu, R., & Suthers, D. (2007). Culture and computers: A review of the concept of culture and implications for intercultural collaborative online learning. *Intercultural Collaboration, 4568*, 260–275.
Vatrapu, R., & Suthers, D. (2010). Intra-and inter-cultural usability in computer-supported collaboration. *Journal of Usability Studies, 5*(4), 172–197.
Vygotsky, L. S. (1978). *Mind in society: The development of higher psychological processes*. Cambridge: Harvard University Press.
Wang, M. (2007). Designing online courses that effectively engage learners from diverse cultural backgrounds. *British Journal of Educational Technology, 38*(2), 294–311.
Wang, H. C., Fussell, S. F., & Setlock, L. D. (2009). Cultural difference and adaptation of communication styles in computer-mediated group brainstorming. In *Proceedings of the 27th international conference on Human factors in computing systems* (pp. 669–678). ACM.
Wang, C. M., & Reeves, T. C. (2007). The meaning of culture in online education: Implications for teaching, learning, and design. In A. Edmundson (Ed.), *Globalized e-learning cultural challenges* (pp. 1–17). Hershey: Information Science Publishing.
Western Interstate Commission for Higher Education Cooperative for Educational Technology (WCET). (2010). *Managing online education survey*. Retrieved January 4, 2012 from http://wcet.wiche.edu/advance/managing-online-education-survey.
Whorf, B. E. (1956). Selected writings of Benjamin Lee Whorf. In J. B. Carroll (ed.), *Language, thought and reality*. Cambridge, MA: MIT Press.
Willey, M. M. (1929). The validity of the culture concept. *The American Journal of Sociology, 35*(2), 204–219.
Wong, L. F., & Trinidad, S. G. (2004). Using web-based distance learning to reduce cultural distance. *The Journal of Interactive Online Learning, 3*(1), 1–13.
Wyatt, G. (2005). Satisfaction, academic rigor and interaction: Perceptions of online instruction. *Education, 125*(3), 460–468.
Yammiyavar, P., Clemmensen, T., & Kumar, J. (2008). Influence of cultural background on nonverbal communication in a usability testing situation. *International Journal of Design, 2*(2), 31–40.
Zepke, N., & Leach, L. (2002). Appropriate pedagogy and technology in a cross-cultural distance education context. *Teaching in Higher Education, 7*(3), 309–321.

Chapter 2
Multicultural and Intergenerational Teaching and Learning: Current Research

Little empirical research is available about online college teaching and learning across culture or age. Research is needed to ascertain learning environment pedagogies that positively impact a diversity of students in online contexts. Because collegiate instruction, including online forms, is often culturally based in Germanic- and English-based traditions of American higher education (Chávez & Guido-DiBrito, 1999; Chávez, Ke, & Herrera, 2012; Ibarra, 2001; Rich, 1993; Tisdell, 1995), it is important to conduct research on all types of instruction across the more diverse cultural, age, and other identities of learners (Chávez, 2011; Tisdell, 1995). This review of literature covers areas of study found to some extent in the literature including constructs of culture in higher education, nontraditional student success and intergenerational online instruction, and cross-cultural online education, as well as overviews of methodologies, populations studied, research questions of focus, and major findings.

Constructs of Culture in Higher Education

Higher education in the United States is traditionally structured around individualistic, linear, mind-focused, time-to-task-oriented cultural constructs far from the collective, circular, relational, mind-body-spirit-heart cultural constructs of most ethnic minority students (Brayboy & Maughan, 2009; Chávez et al., 2012; Ibarra, 2001; Rendón, 2009). Unlike epistemological frameworks such as Chicana feminist notions of teaching and learning, collegiate learning constructs rarely include knowledge or activities similar to those in home communities of most students of color (Delgado Bernal, 2001; Elenes, Delgado Bernal, Gonzáles, Trinidad, & Villenas, 2000). Further, these cultural norms are rarely considered strengths or "cultural wealth" that students bring with them into collegiate learning environments (Villalpando &

DOI 10.1007/978-1-4614-0863-5_2,

Solórzano, 2005). Instead, students of color and their ways of learning and being are often viewed from a deficit rather than a strengths approach (Chávez et al., 2012). Individual faculty practice as both cultural insiders and cultural outsiders to the students they teach, sharing similar cultural constructs with some students and different ones with others (Guido-DiBrito & Chávez, 2003).

Culture permeates teaching and learning in all types of instruction (Chávez, 2007; Fried, 1994; Ibarra, 2001; Johns & Kelley Sipp, 2004; Rendón, 2009). Face-to-face and technology-mediated learning environment designs are infused with cultural values, norms, and assumptions (Branch, 1997; McLoughlin & Oliver, 2000). Learning difficulties are likely to arise when underlying pedagogical values, norms, and epistemologies in one ethnic population are culturally inappropriate or ineffective in another (e.g., Collis, 1999; Ibarra, 2001; Reeves & Reeves, 1997). Ethnic populations of students who are farthest from cultural epistemologies common in current instructional norms also retain and graduate at the lowest rates in college nationally (Almanac of Higher Education, 2007a, 2007b; Ibarra, 2001). Faculty and students are usually unaware of how culture manifests in teaching and learning (Tisdell, 1995; Weinstein & Obear, 1992). Domestic and international students of color experience very real challenges in negotiating academic norms based in cultures not their own (Guido-DiBrito & Chávez, 2003; Ibarra, 2001; Viernes Turner, 1994).

There is little research on cross-cultural pedagogy for college students in classroom (Chávez, 2011) or web-based (Henderson, 1996; Ke, Chávez, & Herrera, 2009) learning contexts. In an extensive review of research on culture in collegiate teaching and learning, we found limited, though important, studies on cultural dimensions for learning including the relationship between learner racial/cultural demographics and learning outcomes (Gurin, Dey, Hurtado, & Gurin, 2002), cultural self-awareness of the learning facilitator (Tisdell, 1995; Weinstein & Obear, 1992), intersections of identity and learning (Chávez & Guido-DiBrito, 1999; Guido-DiBrito & Chávez, 2003), learning environment climate (Chávez, 2007; Chesler, Lewis, & Crowfoot, 2005), diverse motivations across cultures (Heine et al., 2001), silence and reflection in teaching and learning (Covarrubias & Windchief, 2009), and cross-cultural pedagogies (Bennett & Bennett, 1994; Ibarra, 2001). With some notable exceptions, few researchers seem to build on their own work, few studies build on the work of other researchers, and studies are rarely linked across the literature (Chávez, 2011).

Larger frameworks on intersections of culture and teaching/learning are rare in the literature with a few notable exceptions. One body of work on cultural constructs, paradigms, and epistemologies deeply expresses the contextual, relational, spiritual, holistic, and pragmatic nature of teaching and learning found across diverse Native American worldviews (Cajete, 1994). Delgado Bernal (2001) frames a Mestiza epistemology of Chicana college students studied through Anzaldúa's (1987) work. This study addresses the criticality of spirituality, collectivity, and connections to cultural communities in relation to learning, success, and retention. Chávez (2007) empirically derived a model of six teaching elements from a study of four collegiate classrooms identified by international and domestic students of color as multiculturally empowering.

Cross-Cultural Online Education

We conducted a recent literature search of cross-cultural online education within the data pool of computerized bibliographic databases (i.e., ERIC, PsycInfo, Educational Research Complete, Dissertation Abstracts, ACM), major education and technology journals, conference proceedings, and the reference lists of several reviews. During the literature search process, the keywords used included "culture," "minority," "online learning," and "distance education" (and variations of these terms). The data research resulted in the finding of 44 quality articles on cross-cultural online education, which either provided a rich description of the theoretical framework or presented infield research data as an empirical study paper. Of the 44 cross-cultural articles, 22 focused on the online learning experiences and perceptions of students of different cultures, and 26 explored the development of cross-cultural online instruction from an institutional or pedagogical point of view (Appendix Table 2.1).

Of the 22 articles on cross-cultural online learning experiences, many concentrated on learning experiences of Asian students (e.g., Chinese, Japanese, Korean, Indian, & Malaysian) in comparison to that of Anglo students. Fewer studies examined African or Hispanic/Latino students and even less examine experiences of Native American students. Populations differ in student status as well. A majority of populations explored in the literature were graduate students or professionals who worked full time with a few studies of undergraduate students and one conducted at the high school level. Students in reviewed studies were recruited most often from education courses, with only a few from medicine, business, language, music, and religion.

The literature of cross-cultural online learning consistently indicates culturally related diversity. Many scholars found students' thoughts and actions at odds with regular online learning practices, and forms of communication used online were often incongruent with especially minority student cultures and language. Different reasons were offered for this incongruence. Some studies attribute differences to high-context/low-context cultural norms (Ibarra, 2000; Tu, 2001; Wang, 2007), some attributed it to an inherent conflict between the individualism of online pedagogy and collectivism of many students' cultural values (Adeoye & Wentling, 2007; Anakwe, Kessler, & Christensen, 1999), and others ascribed barriers to fundamental differences in student beliefs about the nature of knowledge and how one acquires knowledge (Chen, Bennett, & Maton, 2008; Makoe, 2006). Correspondingly, recommendations for the design of culturally responsive pedagogy focus on student needs at the micro level considering variables such as language, learning styles and preferences, sociocultural context, and technological infrastructure. On the other hand, Van den Branden and Lambert (1999) challenge the notion of student culture at the micro level altogether, arguing that the online learning environment also creates its own culture or society. Sang (2007) argued that online environments should be adapted and redeveloped to avoid cultural imperialism and Anglo-Saxon dominance. This is not just culturally responsive online pedagogy but ethically responsive pedagogy and moves beyond issues of culture into issues about what is ethical in online learning (Anderson & Simpson, 2007). Notably, the review of literature indicated that there is an absence of empirical research on cross-cultural online learning. Theoretical propositions or conceptual papers dominate the literature of cross-cultural online learning.

The 26 studies on cross-cultural online instruction can be grouped into two areas related to online course design and delivery: issues raised by online instruction as it relates to students' culture and language (e.g., Anderson & Simpson, 2007; Lauzon, 1999; McLaren, 2007; Sang, 2007; Van den Branden & Lambert, 1999) and design and implementation of specific modes of online instruction to address student cultural ways of learning and interaction (e.g., Adams & Sean Evans, 2004; Dahl, 2004; Johari, 2005; Kumar & Bhattacharya, 2007; Llambi et al., 2008; McLoughlin, 1999; Rasmussen, Nichols & Ferguson, 2006; Smith & Ayers, 2006).

The primary population in the literature of cross-cultural instruction is still graduate and professional students who major in education. A few articles examine curriculum of undergraduate students by focusing on programs for new students via introductory or bridge programs (Arias, 2000; McLoughlin & Oliver, 2000; Smith & Ayers, 2006). The majority of articles have not addressed course content at all (Amant, 2002; Anderson & Simpson, 2007; Arias, 2000; Johari, 2005; Lauzon, 1999; Lin, 2007; McLaren, 2007; McLoughlin, 1999; Rasmussen et al., 2006; Sang, 2007). Instead, authors explored the pedagogical and interactive needs and adaptations necessary to address students' culture, which could be a specific culture, such as Arab or Maori, or referred to a general "minority" or nontraditional student culture in the online learning environment, regardless of course content.

The articles reviewed discussed general approaches to guide the design of culturally responsive learning environments and shared common features, such as using student-centered learning systems to support and engage students and creating constructivist online environments that are explicit and equitable. Recommendations focused on student needs in terms of language, learning styles and preferences, sociocultural context, and technological infrastructure. For example, Johari (2005) discussed how designers can integrate eight differentials in preparing online instructional materials and apply strategies to match learners to suitable courses. He provides two checklists distilled from research "Six recommendations for low-context (US) instructional designers" and "Eight recommendations designers should make for their high-context students."

Some of this literature goes beyond general principles and recommendations for culturally responsive instructional design and offers more specific examples and suggestions based on actual programs or courses studied. Zepke and Leach (2002), for instance, suggested integration of a narrative line, opportunities for face-to-face interaction, and content and materials that represent (Maori) students' culture. Henderson (1996) presented one of the most comprehensive analyses. Her *Multiple Cultural Pedagogic Model* of interactive multimedia instructional design is based in turn on the 14 dimensions of interactive learning of Reeves (1992). Reeves' 14 dimensions include several highly likely to differ among different cultures, for example, pedagogical philosophy (instructivism vs. constructivist), goal orientation (sharply focused vs. unfocused), role of instructor (teacher proof vs. equalitarian facilitator), value of errors (errorless learning vs. learning from experience), motivation (extrinsic vs. intrinsic), accommodation of individual differences (nonexistent vs. multifaceted), learner control (nonexistent vs. unrestricted), and cooperative learning (unsupported vs. integral). Henderson's key addition to Reeves' set of dimensions is the idea of incorporating multiple cultural perspectives into an *eclectic paradigm*, so that multiple cultures maintain their identities and can have their respective cultures accommodated. This in turn requires that both ends of each dimension must be taken into account in the course design and context. She also argues that Reeves' choice of endpoint values, at least for the dimension Epistemology, may in turn be based on Western notions or theories of the nature of learning and knowledge and argues that different endpoints can be defined based on Asian or Australian Aboriginal epistemologies. In any case, different profiles based on these dimensions may be optimal for different cultural groups, and they may also vary within the timeline of a learning experience itself (e.g., an instructivist pedagogy at some points and a constructivist at others).

Modes and Focus of Research

Research Methods

Of the 40 articles collected on cross-cultural online education, the most common methodology utilized was case study (refer to Table 2.1). Overall there were 17 qualitative studies, nine quantitative studies, two mixed methods, and 12 theoretical or propositional discussions. Of the 17 qualitative articles, 15 were case studies, one used a phenomenological approach, and the other was an ethnography study.

Case studies varied in cultural focus, examining cross-cultural students' online education from around the globe. Student populations included Latino (Ibarra, 2000), Native American (Adams & Sean Evans, 2004; Berkshire & Smith, 2000), Maori (Zepke & Leach, 2002), South African (Makoe, 2006), Chinese (Chen et al., 2008; Chen, Mashhadi, Ang, & Harkrider, 1999; Hurd & Xiao, 2006), the Netherlands (Collis, 1999), Cyprus (Zembylas, 2008), the United Kingdom (Crane, 2005; Dillon, Wang, & Tearle, 2007; Hurd & Xiao, 2006; McGivney, 2004), as well as diverse nontraditional students in the United States (Evans et al., 2007; Shenk, Moore, & Davis, 2004) and abroad (Venter, 2003).

While the population in each study differed, almost all case studies focused on student performance and experience in some way. An example was a case study conducted by Venter (2003), in which the researcher examined different coping strategies used by 43 adult students involved in a 2-year master's program delivered globally via distance learning. The student enrollment in the program was broadly grouped from European to Asian Pacific background. The study explored interactions between strategies used to cope with isolation and culture and the connections between student culture and learning style.

Unlike the qualitative articles where case study stood out as the most dominant methodology, in the quantitative research articles, a variety of methodologies were used to investigate cross-cultural online education, including surveys (Anakwe et al., 1999; Buerck, Malmstrom, & Peppers, 2003; Chernish, DeFranco, Lindner, & Dooley, 2005; Yong & Parrella, 2004), the use of pre- and posttests (Chernish et al., 2005; Chyung, 2007), questionnaires (Makoe, Richardson, & Price, 2008), data analysis of student records, and/or examination of online activity (Angiello, 2002; Chyung, 2007; Patton, 2000; Stafford & Lindsey, 2007). Student populations in quantitative studies were not as diverse as those studied using qualitative methods with most focusing on online students in the United States. However, nontraditional, older students were more likely to be studied using a quantitative method. A typical example of a study using quantitative methodologies is Anakwe's et al. (1999). In this study, the researcher employed the use of surveys to examine distance learning orientations of 424 students enrolled at two northeastern universities. Similar to the qualitative example offered above, connections between student culture and learning styles are part of the findings in this study.

Theoretical or propositional papers were the second most common type of publication found on the topic of web-based cross-cultural education. Studies either focused on the role of diverse cultures online in general terms (Anderson & Simpson, 2007; Arias, 2000; Lauzon, 1999; McLoughlin & Oliver, 2000; Rasmussen et al., 2006) or spoke of issues related to a specific population such as Indigenous Australians (McLoughlin, 1999), the Arab world (McLaren, 2007), Europe (Van den Branden & Lambert, 1999), Hispanic/Latino-Americans (Smith & Ayers, 2006), students in Hong Kong (Sang, 2007) or Native American women (Dahl, 2004).

Of the 12 theoretical/propositional articles examined, nine focused on the design of culturally relevant curriculum, two were critiques of learning-related cultural constructs and dimensions, and one focused on implications for program development. A typical theoretical examination of online curriculum related to culture was conducted by McLoughlin and Oliver (2000). In this chapter, the author explored different ways educational designers can ensure inclusivity in the curricular design process. A case is made for equitable educational planning via design that addresses social and cultural dimensions of learning.

The two mixed-method studies are similar to previously discussed studies; each focuses on the online student experience with a particular emphasis on student perceptions. One study explored interactions between adult professional learners in the United States (Rhode, 2009), while the other focused on issues of power between teachers, students, and peers in distance learning courses across the United States, China, and South Korea (Wang, 2007). Both studies found significant differences between cultural groups and students' online learning experiences.

Populations Studied

Upon deeper examination of populations represented in the previous discussion, some trends appear. Key terms and topics utilized for purposes of this review are important here. Topics of distance learning and online education were searched in combination with culture and nontraditional students. "Culture" in the context of this literature review was further broken down in subsequent searches to include specific populations of students including Latino/Latina, Hispanic, African American, and Native American. Furthermore, nontraditional students were also a component of this search and appear to make up the largest populations.

In relation to culture, the two largest populations studied were Chinese and Latino/Hispanic students. Many studies explored interactions between a variety of cultures as they progressed through online courses together in the United States or abroad. Studies exploring multiple cultures in the context of an online learning course were the norm with the majority of these diverse populations dwelling in the United States and the UK.

Research Questions

Of the literature reviewed, types of questions asked by researchers were quite similar. Questions about student interactions, feelings, perceptions, performance, and traits were common. For example, in the quantitative study by Zepke and Leach (2002), researchers investigated the following questions: (1) Would an individual's culture affect his or her receptivity toward distance learning? (2) Would an individual's culture affect his or her preference for particular distance learning media? (3) Would an individual's culture affect his or her preference for distance learning in a particular course type? One example with a similar focus is a case study by Dillon et al. (2007) who questioned how in a defined educational situation learning behaviors would differ across cultures and what the implications of these differences were for online communication.

Inquiry into challenges or problems in relation to student culture and age was also common, as were questions about strategies used by students to overcome such challenges when learning online. For example, the study by Hurd and Xiao (2006) examined the perceptions and goals of UK and Chinese students in distance language courses, specific problems they encountered as they studied, and strategies they used to address them, and the ways students from these two cultures differed with respect to these factors.

Of the articles examined for this literature review, the most common theme of inquiry was the issue of culturally relevant curriculum. Specifically, more studies examined the ways curriculum and pedagogy either met the needs or should change in order to better meet the needs of students based on their culture and background. For example, in a case study, Collis (1999) posed the following research question: How can WWW-based course-support sites and systems be designed to offer optimal flexibility in terms of culture-related differences in its users? Almost all of the theoretical and propositional articles in our review share this type of curricular focus in the central theme of their discussion.

Major Findings

Findings presented in this cross-section of literature can be grouped into two broad categories: (1) relationship between student culture and the effectiveness of distance education as a delivery method and (2) relationships between student culture, learning style, and instructional design. The most common type of findings and/or themes came from studies that addressed connections between students' culture and learning style and the development of online curriculum and pedagogy. For these studies, researchers argued that online learning environment, learning content, and pedagogy must be approached culturally, critically, and ethically in order to accommodate the needs of students. They explored ways in which conceptions of learning are culturally and contextually dependent and consequently how students' cultural background, language, learning styles, and problem-solving strategies impact distance education experiences.

For example, in the study by Chen et al. (1999), researchers argued for online curriculum designed and delivered to create culturally mediated social interaction. Because students' experiences of culture and technology play a key role in learning, the authors state that social and cultural understandings must be made explicit through accessibility, interconnectivity, immediacy, interactivity, and integration in curriculum design. In other articles, learning styles are discussed in relation to student culture. For example, Anakwe et al. (1999) discussed the relationship between culture and the individualist versus collectivist orientation of learners, and Buerck et al. (2003) explored relationships between student culture and the assimilator versus converger learning styles. Yong and Parrella (2004) associated these traits with independent versus dependent learner styles.

The most critical findings argue that practices and approaches used in distance learning courses are often at odds with ways of thinking, acting, and being that students bring with them. Chen et al. (2008) argued that the challenges Chinese learners experience online have roots in basic beliefs about the nature of knowledge and knowledge accumulation. Dillon et al. (2007) saw design and implementation of online communications act as major barriers because of differing cultural and language differences. In the ethnographic study, Knight, Dixon, Norton, and Bentley (2004) investigated the use of technology with Black and Latino/Latina students in a New York City high school. They posited that students may be subjected to the same oppressive pedagogies of traditional classrooms when using technology if practitioners fail to approach such pedagogies and curriculum critically.

The second broad category of findings identified through this literature review is relationships between age- or ethnicity-related culture and the effectiveness of distance learning methods. Previous studies presented varied and seemingly contradictory findings. For example, Chyung (2007) stated that older students are more active than younger students online, and Stafford and Lindsey (2007) argued that nontraditional students are more likely to benefit from a distance learning format. In contrast, McGivney (2004) argued that nontraditional students are less likely to stay in distance learning programs overtime. Buerck et al. (2003) found differences in performance between traditional and nontraditional students that can be attributed to differences in learning styles. However, Evans et al. (2007) found no difference in performance between traditional and nontraditional students. Finally, Angiello (2002) found that Hispanic students are not as successful as other students when taking online learning courses, while Van den Branden and Lambert (1999) suggested that online culture trumps students' individual culture in the distance education environment.

Overall, current literature points to the need for more comprehensive empirical studies that cross academic disciplines, student cultural populations, a diversity of pedagogical designs, and quantitative and qualitative modes of research.

Nontraditional Student Success and Intergenerational Online Education

Research on collegiate teaching and learning is predominantly based in historical perspectives, beliefs, and curriculum of a traditional student profile – of a person who is northern European Caucasian, 17–24 years old, and living on or near campus (Kasworm & Pike, 1994). Contemporary student populations diverge significantly from these student profiles and experiences. Nontraditional students now comprise approximately 40 % of the postsecondary population and nearly 78 % receive education in web-based distance format (Kuenzi, 2008). Corresponding to nontraditional students' learning profiles, adaptive web-based teaching and learning design interventions should be identified through in situ studies.

Yet a recent review on nontraditional/adult students in online learning settings indicated only 13 scholarly articles that focus on student experience or the pedagogical dimensions for age-related online learning. Of the 13, nine focus on intergenerational learning (Benson & Samarawickrema, 2007; Buerck et al., 2003; Chyung, 2007; de Lange, Waldmann, & Wyatt, 1997; Makoe et al., 2008; McGivney, 2004; Rhode, 2009; Shinkareva & Benson, 2007; Stafford & Lindsey, 2007) and five focus on intergenerational instruction (Crane, 2005; Davis, 2006; McGivney, 2004; McPatton, 2000; Sorensen & Murchú, 2004) with one article falling into both categories (McGivney, 2004). In the following section, population, methodology, research questions, and major findings of these articles will be discussed in detail (Appendix Table 2.2).

Nontraditional or Adult Student Population Studied

In the 13 articles reviewed, the population was described as "nontraditional" or "adult" students; however, almost every article varied in its definition of these terms. Differing criteria were used across studies to explain features of and/or define a nontraditional or adult student. Most commonly, authors based determinations on student age, gender, and employment status. More recently, definitions have also included parental status and returning to school. This variation in definitions and criteria makes research in this area difficult to compare.

For example, when referring to student age, the following criteria were listed as determinants for "nontraditional" or adult student status: mean age 36 (Zembylas, 2008), ages 31–45 (Shinkareva & Benson, 2007), mean age 40 (Chyung, 2007), ages 25–34 (Stafford & Lindsey, 2007), age 22+ (Buerck et al., 2003), ages 25–40 (Crane, 2005), over 25 (McGivney, 2004), and mean age 32 (de Lange et al., 1997). Based on this grouping, it would appear a nontraditional or adult student is not younger than 22 years of age. Though less often considered, student gender was also used to define the nontraditional or adult student. In 4 of the 13 studies (Crane, 2005; de Lange et al., 1997; Shinkareva & Benson, 2007; Zembylas, 2008), the majority of students under study were female, and gender was considered a factor in determining nontraditional student status.

The criteria for adult or nontraditional student status vary greatly in the articles, with some overlap. Most often a nontraditional student was defined as one who is new to higher education (Crane, 2005; Davis, 2006; de Lange et al., 1997; Makoe et al., 2008; Patton, 2000; Shinkareva & Benson, 2007), new to distance learning (Crane, 2005; Makoe et al., 2008; McPatton, 2000), and/or new to the subject area or program (Makoe et al., 2008; McPatton, 2000; Shinkareva & Benson, 2007). Similarly, student status may be described as it relates to professional or job status, whereas a nontraditional/adult student is one who has been working full time for 3 or more years (Buerck et al., 2003), is working toward a professional development certificate (Rhode, 2009), has a gap since being in school full time (Davis, 2006; McGivney, 2004), is employed full time as a professional (Shinkareva & Benson, 2007; Sorensen & Murchú, 2004; Zembylas, 2008), or has returned to school to improve employability (McPatton, 2000). One study also defined students based on geography including rural and international student status as criteria (Patton, 2000).

Of the previous studies on intergenerational online learning experiences or web-based intergenerational instruction, populations under study were predominantly Western with the majority from the United States (e.g., Buerck et al., 2003; Chyung, 2007; Davis, 2006; McGivney, 2004; Rhode, 2009; Shinkareva & Benson, 2007; Stafford & Lindsey, 2007), with three from the United Kingdom (Crane, 2005; Makoe et al., 2008; McGivney, 2004), one each from Cyprus (Zembylas, 2008) and Australia (de Lange et al., 1997), and one study compared Ireland and Denmark (Sorensen & Murchú, 2004).

Research Questions

In articles on intergenerational online learning, authors investigated the behaviors, preferences, interactions, dispositions, and performance of students in the distance education environment. These articles examined students' conceptions of learning (e.g., Makoe et al., 2008), how they talk about emotions online (e.g., Zembylas, 2008), or rates of retention compared to younger students (e.g., McGivney, 2004). In Chyung's (2007) quantitative study, the author investigated how age and gender affect online behavior, self-efficacy, and academic performance in the online learning environment. In Rhode's (2009) mixed-method study, the author investigated forms of interaction adult learners engaged in and valued most in online courses and how adults perceived the impact of peer interaction on their self-paced online experience.

In the articles about web-based intergenerational instruction, authors examined learning environment and pedagogy as they were developed and/or used with nontraditional/adult students in distance education. They also investigated the impact of instructional practice and behavior (Patton, 2000) as well as the effectiveness of a specific online program, course, or seminar (Crane, 2005; Davis, 2006; McGivney, 2004; Sorensen & Murchú, 2004). For example, Crane (2005) examined and described how the implementation of an online program was successful in retaining students and widening educational access to nontraditional students. The online program success factors reported include the use of tutors, guidance, staff development, and providing the curriculum in a range of formats for students.

Research Methods

Unlike the dominant use of qualitative methodology (i.e., case study) found in the literature of cross-cultural online learning, the literature of intergenerational learning is predominantly quantitative in methodology. Of the nine articles reviewed, six are quantitative and one uses mixed methods (Rhode, 2009). Of the quantitative studies, four are survey studies (Buerck et al., 2003; de Lange et al., 1997; Makoe et al., 2008; Shinkareva & Benson, 2007), and two are data/content analysis (Chyung, 2007; Stafford & Lindsey, 2007). The remaining two articles were case studies (McGivney, 2004; Zembylas, 2008).

A typical survey study was conducted by Buerck et al.'s (2003), who investigated the relationship between nontraditional students' preferred learning environment (i.e., face-to-face or online) and their learning styles. The authors surveyed 29 nontraditional students enrolled in a computer science class on their self-reported learning styles and learning environment preferences.

The literature of web-based intergenerational instruction is predominantly theoretical, similar to that of web-based cross-cultural instruction. Of the five articles found, three are theoretical (Crane, 2005; Davis, 2006; Sorensen & Murchú, 2004), one is content/data analysis (Patton, 2000), and one is case study (McGivney, 2004). A typical theoretical paper by Davis (2006) discussed the design of an introductory student seminar for adult students new to the College of Liberal Studies. Davis investigated how to design a course that strengthened students' general writing ability while integrating disciplines in a way that was engaging to new students. He structured the course into four units and incorporated real-world activities to introduce key concepts in the humanities, natural, and social sciences.

Major Findings

Findings of prior studies on intergenerational learning support the notion that learning is culturally and contextually dependent, particularly for adult students in online learning environments. For example, Makoe et al. (2008) stated that conceptions of learning derived from the experience, context, and culture of the adult learner. Zembylas (2008) found that emotional responses differed online based on social and gender roles and responsibilities of the participant. When examining online participation for nontraditional students, Rhode (2009) found that not all interactions were considered equally effective or valued and that informal interactions were just as important as formal interactions for the nontraditional student. Older students were found to post more often than younger students (Chyung, 2007) and were more likely to have a converger learning style (Buerck et al., 2003). Oftentimes, the successful online adult learners were reported to have a higher self-directed learning ability and IT skills, leading to improved effort, self-efficacy, and motivation (Shinkareva & Benson, 2007).

Though limited, prior research on intergenerational instruction has contributed a list of generic heuristics or specific suggestions on how to design online learning environments to meet the needs of nontraditional/adult learners. Specifically, researchers recommend flexibility with deadlines and other learning activity requirements so that adult learners are more likely to complete assignments and be successful in the course (Patton, 2000). McGivney (2004) suggested that adult learners also need more time in general to complete their online classes than their younger "traditional" counterparts and they are more likely to complete the course and/or program if given more time. Other recommendations for instructional design include dividing courses into smaller units (Davis, 2006), using real-world activities that are engaging (Davis, 2006; Sorensen & Murchú, 2004), and constructing an online environment that facilitates community (Sorensen & Murchú, 2004).

Acknowledgements The authors would like to thank Michelle Jewett for her research assistance and brilliant insights.

Appendix

Table 2.1 A synthesis of reviewed articles on cross-cultural online education

Study	Method	Sample and site	Subject content	Uni- or multicultural	Cultural dimensions	Culture-related education dimension[a]	Findings or propositions
Adams and Sean Evans (2004)	Case study	Native American graduate students taking online courses from the reservation	Education	Uni-cultural	Ethnicity: Navajo	Adaptation: Providing library service for online courses	In-person instruction on library search being most effective and culturally respectful form Observational and collaborative learning activities Culturally sensitive materials (e.g., videos depicting successful stories of Native American)
Adeoye and Wentling (2007)	Survey and user observation with correlation analyses	30 attendees of an international workshop	Training improvement	Multicultural	National culture: Power distance, Individualism/ collectivism, femininity/ masculinity, uncertainty avoidance	Inclusion/comparison: Usability of e-learning system	High PDI correlated with higher learning satisfaction and more errant mouse clicks, uncertainty avoidance correlated with learnability time
Anakwe et al. (1999)	Survey and correlation analyses	424 students at two NE universities: mean age 25; 79 % undergrads, 43 % male, 8 % African American, 14 % Asian, 61 % Caucasian, 7 % Hispanic, 1 % Native American	Management courses	Multicultural	Ethnicity culture: individualism/ collectivism	Inclusion: Perceptions and preferences of a distance learning environment	Individualists prefer interactive medium of communication while collectivists prefer a face-to-face interaction for a long-term relationship Individualists would consider DL for major course types while collectivists consider DL for non-relationship course type

(continued)

Table 2.1 (continued)

Study	Method	Sample and site	Subject content	Uni- or multicultural	Cultural dimensions	Culture-related education dimension[a]	Findings or propositions
Anderson and Simpson (2007)	Theoretical discussion	N/A	Online courses and distance education, in general	Multicultural	Generic	Inclusion: Design strategies on multicultural learning environment	Viewing culture not only as dispositions brought to the online class but also the pedagogical culture produced out of online interactions
Angiello (2002)	Secondary data analysis (academic records), survey, *t*-test of GPAs	113,860 student records from online courses at a New Jersey community college: surveys with 49 distance education students	N/A	Uni-cultural	Ethnicity: Hispanic	Comparison: GPA and online class enrollment	Hispanics were more disadvantaged online when compared to Whites
Bentley, Tinney, and Chia (2005)	Theoretical discussion	International students and curriculum designers participating in cross-cultural online instruction	N/A	Multicultural	Generic	Inclusion: Culture-related factors that influences learners' perceptions of online learning	Eight factors: language, educational culture, technical infrastructure, primary audience, learning styles, reasoning patterns, cultural context, and social context
Berkshire and Smith (2000)	Case study	Rural Alaska Native adult students (age 28+) in online program at Alaska Pacific University	Business Administration, human services and teacher education	Uni-cultural	Ethnicity: Alaska Native American	Adaptation: Online course design for a special learner group	Cultural appropriate design features: Asynchronous discussion with weekly online chat Inductive and application-based knowledge building Minimal technology requirement

Bloomberg (2007)	Case study	22 graduate students (aged 25–55) and 10 faculty in a Jewish distance learning program	Jewish education and Judaic studies	Uni-cultural	Ethnicity: Jewish	Adaptation: Perceptions of learning community within a videoconference-based learning program	Not all students had expectations of being part of a learning community but were able to identify community Acknowledged the key roles of instructor and technology
Chen et al. (1999)	Case study	3 Singapore based learning systems in 3 different contexts: local-institutional, trans-institutional, and global	2 systems used for student teachers, 1 collaborative learning science project with secondary students	Uni-cultural	Nationality: Singaporean	Adaptation: Culturally adaptive learning program design	Programs are successful
Chen et al. (2008)	Case study (interview, questionnaire, and document analysis)	2 Chinese female, English teachers taking online master courses	Education	Uni-cultural	Nationality: from heritage culture (Chinese) to host culture (USA)	Acculturation: Acculturation process in online learning environments	Acculturation challenges: reduced input from the instructor, absence of student-teacher relationship, behavioral shifts
Collis (1999)	Theoretical discussion	N/A	Generic	Multicultural	Comprehensive	Inclusion: Multicultural online instructional design	A list of culture-related dimensions of an online learning environment

(continued)

Table 2.1 (continued)

Study	Method	Sample and site	Subject content	Uni- or multicultural	Cultural dimensions	Culture-related education dimension[a]	Findings or propositions
Dillon et al. (2007)	Situation analysis (interpretive research)	5 British and 23 international students in the UK	Doctoral education course: nature of educational enquiry	Multicultural	National culture: high/low context, individualism/collectivism, affirmative/deferential language	Inclusion: Factors lead to cultural disconnection in the online learning environment	Cultural disconnection (different learning styles, forms of communication, and personal expectations) is an interaction between outer culture characteristics (national culture), inner culture characteristics (individual personality), and the educational environment Advocating learners codesign a culturally adaptive educational environment
Gunawardena et al. (2001)	Survey and focus group interview	50 online students from a US university (aged 40–49) and 50 online students from a Mexico university (aged 23–53)	N/A	Multicultural	National culture: USA and Mexico (power distance, collectivism/individualism, language), individual culture (gender and technological competency), and academic culture (time frame of virtual groups)	Inclusion: Culture on students' perceptions of online group development processes	Culture factors influenced online group process and development
Hedberg and Brown (2002)	Artifact analysis	15 postgraduate educational design students from Hong Kong	Cognition and interface design	Uni-cultural	National culture: Chinese	Adaptation: Cultural interpretation of the visual information	Cultural differences in meaning and representation in the interface design

Henning (2003)	Narrative case study	6 first time adult e-learners in Master's of Education program at a South African university	Qualitative research and writing composition	Uni-cultural	National culture: South Africa	Adaptation: Distributed cognition in a global online learning environment	The cognition is contained or situated in non-global, culture-specific discourse of local learners
Hogan (2009)	Evaluation study (survey and focus group interview)	A distance learning program delivered to 12 Pacific island countries	N/A	Uni-cultural	National culture: Pacific island countries	Adaptation: Effectiveness of the online learning program for Pacific students	Student cusses and satisfaction were lower for online students Culture and skill level (typing and computer skills) caused some students to prefer correspondence courses than online delivery
Hurd and Xiao (2006)	Case study	204 Open University (UK) students ages 35–50; 170 SRTVU (China) students in their 1930s	Language learning	Multicultural	National culture: English and Chinese	Inclusion: Culture on perceptions of online learning	Learning strategies used by students reflected their culture: Higher levels of self-awareness among Chinese students, related to a tradition of reflective practice in Chinese culture Lower levels of Chinese students of key aspects of autonomy, linked to a culture of dependence on the teacher as the sole authority Spontaneous action of Chinese students in comparison to advanced planning of British students

(continued)

Table 2.1 (continued)

Study	Method	Sample and site	Subject content	Uni- or multicultural	Cultural dimensions	Culture-related education dimension[a]	Findings or propositions
Hudson, Hudson, and Steel (2006)	Ethnography	10 students in an international online master's program of the Netherlands and the UK	Digital media applications	Multicultural	National culture: Dutch and English	Comparison: Culture on collaboration in an international online learning community	The awareness of cultural differences: preferred formats of interaction and communication, subtleties of language
Ibarra (2000)	Case study	7 Latino/Latina students in graduate level distance learning programs at Walden University	N/A	Uni-cultural	Ethnicity: Latino: low context/high context	Adaptation: Culture on perceptions of online learning	Higher education environment must be designed to have a good balance of high- and low-context culture
Knight et al. (2004)	Ethnography	Cross-aged group of students in grades 9–12; college bound Black and Latino students in NYC	Music education	Multicultural	Ethnicity: Black and Latino Individual culture (age)	Adaptation: Videoconferencing for minority students in online learning	Active learning was shaped by the interaction between videoconferencing, multiple literacies, and traditional pedagogies
Kumar and Bhattacharya (2007)	Case description	e-learning programs in Africa	N/A	Multicultural	National culture: Africa	Inclusion: Successful cases of multicultural e-learning	Program is successful
Lauzon (1999)	Theoretical discussion	Technologically mediated education	N/A	Multicultural	Individual culture: social economic status	Inclusion: The potential of technology to challenge and transgress cultural borders for minority learner groups	Communication technology can enable a mediated education in the format of community of practice to transgress cultural borders

Lea (2001)	Case study (interviewing and score comparison)	147 students, with 32 identified as "other" cultural group students in an online MA program of UK's Open University	N/A	Multicultural	National culture: native speaker versus nonnative speaker	Inclusion/comparison: Cultural and linguistic differences in global online learning environments	Cultural otherness: "Other" students seemed to gain lower average assessment scores Linguistic difference in time taken to respond appropriately, effectiveness in argument, and accurate use of language Academic convention
Lim (2004)	Survey research and comparison analysis	236 Education students attending Korean University and a university in the southwestern USA	N/A	Multicultural	National culture: Korea versus USA; Individual culture (gender)	Comparison: National culture and individual culture on perceived online learning motivation	American students scored significantly higher for the four motivation types (course relevancy, course interest, reinforcement, and self-efficacy) Korean students scored significantly higher for learner control
Lin (2007)	Theoretical discussion	Rural Aboriginal children in Taiwan	N/A	Uni-cultural	Ethnicity: Aboriginal	Adaptation: Culture-related e-learning program development strategies	Tribal-elder-centered participatory design
Llambi et al. (2008)	Mixed method	1,200 physicians in Uruguay	Alzheimer and other dementias adapted using EviDoctor program	Multicultural	National culture: Canadian and Uruguay	Adaptation: Adapt an online course from the Canadian context to Uruguay context	Key concepts learned: Flexibility in determin-ing the content Language, culture of e-learning, and resources to sustain long-term collaboration

(continued)

Table 2.1 (continued)

Study	Method	Sample and site	Subject content	Uni- or multicultural	Cultural dimensions	Culture-related education dimension[a]	Findings or propositions
Makoe (2006)	Interview	5 online learners at the University of South Africa (Black South African, aged 19–34)	N/A	Uni-cultural	Ethnicity: Black South African	Adaptation: Culture/ social inequality on perceptions of online learning	Perceptions of learning was influenced by the social and cultural environment in which one grew up, his level of education, and construal of self in relation to the community
McLaren (2007)	Theoretical discussion	Arab higher education institutions	N/A	Uni-cultural	National culture: Arabic world, religion, gender, and linguistic	Adaptation: Cultural interference/ considerations for e-learning in Arabic world	Cultural interferences for e-learning in Arabic world: Cross-religion, cross-gender socialization/interaction
McLoughlin (1999)	Theoretical discussion	Development of online unit of study for Indigenous learners in Australia	N/A	Multicultural	National culture: Indigenous learner in Australia	Adaptation: E-learning design principles for special learner group	Cross-cultural pedagogical ladder—from monocultural to cross-cultural
McLoughlin and Oliver (2000)	Theoretical discussion	Development of online unit of study for Indigenous learners in Australia	Pathways to Learning (pre-university bridging course)	Multicultural	National culture: Indigenous learner in Australia	Adaptation: e-Learning design principles for special learner group	Advocating flexibility in adaptive course design and community-based collaborative learning
Rasmussen et al. (2006)	Theoretical discussion	Instructional strategies for online multicultural courses	N/A	Multicultural	Generic	Inclusion: Multiculturalism in online education	Orientation strategy, content strategy, interaction strategy, and conclusion strategy

Sanchez, Stuckey, and Morris (1998)	Phenomenology	American Indian tribal communities within USA	N/A	Uni-cultural	Ethnicity: Native American	Adaptation: e-Learning design principles for special learner group	Using new technologies can preserve, maintain, and revitalize traditional languages and cultures
Sang (2007)	Theoretical discussion	e-learning programs used in educational institutions in Hong Kong	N/A	Uni-cultural	National/area culture: Hong Kong	Adaptation: Cross-border delivery of e-learning to Hong Kong	Instead of developing a culturally neutral course, online course for Hong Kong should (1) make adaptations to the original culture, (2) jointly redevelop the course with the overseas provider, and (3) create a different version of the original course by translation to the local language
Selinger (2004)	Evaluation report	11-country Cisco Networking Academy program	Computer networks	Multicultural	National culture	Inclusion: Globalization of e-learning	Instructors' role was pivotal in making the curriculum culturally relevant for students Countries mainly differed in how students were treated, how instructors perceived students, and how instructors perceived their roles

(continued)

Table 2.1 (continued)

Study	Method	Sample and site	Subject content	Uni- or multicultural	Cultural dimensions	Culture-related education dimension[a]	Findings or propositions
Shenk, Moore, and Davis (2004)	Case study	24 students; 6 undergrad, 18 graduate; 2 from India, 1 Vietnamese American, 4 African American, and the remaining White; ages 19–53	Communicating with older persons with Alzheimer's disease	Multicultural	Comprehensive: national culture, individual culture (disciplinary, age, and life experience)	Inclusion: The effectiveness of an online course with multicultural students	The diversity of student backgrounds benefits the learning process
Smith and Ayers (2006)	Theoretical synthesis	Community college learners, esp. Hispanic/Latino	N/A	Uni-cultural	Ethnicity: Latino	Adaptation: Culture-related e-learning program development strategies	Collaborative learning and learning community as the most appropriate learning format to address the diversity
Stockhausen and Kawashima (2002)	Ethnography (focus group interview)	27 Japanese nurses (aged 31–35) taking course via the Japanese Nursing Institute and Griffith University, AU	Reflective practice for nurses	Uni-cultural	National culture: Japanese	Adaptation: Cross-border delivery of e-learning to foreign learner group	Japanese nurses needed to reconcile their previous educational and cultural experiences with new ideas: Cultural reflection, making meaning and accepting challenge; perturbed reflection, "not as it seems" (translation issue) and balancing the conflicts

Tu (2001)	Ethnography (interview and document analysis)	6 Chinese graduate students in the College of Education at a university in the southwestern USA	3 different courses using first class conferencing system	Uni-cultural	National culture: Chinese	Acculturation: Culture on perceptions of online learning (e.g., social presence)	The issue of privacy and the three dimensions of social presence (social context, online communication, and interactivity) should be considered when integrating CMC into multicultural classrooms
Van den Branden and Lambert (1999)	Theoretical discussion	Open distance learning culture in European countries	N/A	Multicultural	National culture: European countries	Inclusion: Transnational online learning in EU	Cultural identity and language management are two key issues for transnational learning model development in EU
Wang (2007)	Mixed methods (survey and qualitative content analysis)	University students from USA, China, and South Korea	N/A	Multicultural	National culture: USA, China, and South Korea (power distance)	Comparison: Perceptions of online learning environments	Korean students ranked highest on perceptions of being equal with instructors, while US learners ranked the lowest No difference in perceptions about rules of conduct in online courses Impact of power distance influence learners comfort level in approaching instructors and peers for help

(continued)

Table 2.1 (continued)

Study	Method	Sample and site	Subject content	Uni- or multicultural	Cultural dimensions	Culture-related education dimension[a]	Findings or propositions
Williams et al. (2001)	Action research	Five instructors from five online classes in USA, England, and Australia	Adult education	Multicultural	National culture: USA, England, and Australia	Inclusion: Strategies to facilitating cross-cultural online discussion groups	Main themes of cross-cultural facilitation: Framing and asking open-ended questions Online group participation, process check, understanding group dynamics, expectation of students, facilitator expectations, and facilitator anxiety
Wu and Teoh (2008)	Quantitative content analysis of the online interaction transcripts	1,451 students enrolled for the same course across 28 learning centers in Shanghai (with an average age of 28.4), and 361 students enrolled in the same course across four learning centers in Malaysia (with an average age of 32.8)	Principles of management	Multicultural	National culture: power distance, individualism, masculinity	Comparison: Types of interactions (i.e., cognitive level and interactee), depth of discussions	Engagement levels of two country's students in different types of interactions reflect the differences between the two countries in the degree of national cultural dimensions Older adults were able to contribute to the discussions in a more elaborated way

Yildiz and Bichelmeyer (2003)	Case study (survey, email, and online interaction transcript analysis)	Two online graduate courses at an American university	Education	Multicultural	Nationality: nonnative English speaker	Adaptation: e-learning for international students (ESL students)	Online course provided ESL students with more opportunities to participate in the discussions than in face-to-face classrooms Culture impact students' comfort with learner-oriented discussions as opposed to teacher-delivered course lectures
Zepke and Leach (2002)	Case study	Curriculum project for Maori teachers in Bachelor of Education degree program	Adult education	Uni-cultural	Nationality: Maori	Adaptation: Culture-related e-learning program development strategies	Adult learning theory

[a]*Culture-related education dimensions:*
Adaptation: adapt course to target culture/learner group
Acculturation: adapt oneself (learner) to host culture/environment
Inclusion: multicultural
Comparison: cross-cultural

Table 2.2 A Synthesis of review articles on intergenerational online education

Study	Methodology	Sample/site	Subject content	Learning or instructional dimensions	Findings or propositions
Buerck et al. (2003)	Survey	29 nontraditional students	Computer Science	Learning style of adult students	Older students were more likely to have a converger learning style
Chyung (2007)	A two-way factorial analysis	81 master's degree students, average age 40: 37 female, 44 male	Education	Age and gender differences in online discussion, self-efficacy improvement, and academic performance	Older students posted significantly more messages but younger students improved self-efficacy significantly more
Crane (2005)	Theoretical	Nontraditional adult students (mostly female, ages 25–40) in England	Multidisciplinary	Features of the web-based distance education program	Generic features and examples on the "best practice" of the e-learning program
Davis (2006)	Theoretical	Design of intro student seminar for University of Oklahoma students new to the College of Liberal Studies	Introduction to academic writing	Online course design	Certain course features described (e.g., structure, authentic learning activities)
de Lange et al. (1997)	Survey	107 Australian business students	Accounting and finance	Equity in education: characteristic of online learners and its relationship with performance	Accessibility of online learning to adult learner; males outperformed females; no ethnicity-related or age-related achievement difference
Makoe et al. (2008)	Questionnaire	372 nontraditional students at the Open University, UK	Multidisciplinary, preparatory courses	Conceptions of learning of adult learners	Conceptions of learning of adult learners are culturally and contextually dependent

McGivney (2004)	Case study	Adult students (over 25) attending Open University in the UK	Unstated	Retention and non-completion patterns of adult students	A list of personal, family, cultural, and instructional factors for non-completion patterns for adult learners
Patton (2000)	Quantitative analysis of student records, grades, dropout rates, etc.	Records of 8 Australian lecturers working with 400 nontraditional students from Southeast Asia	Business	Course design features	Flexibility with assignment deadlines as a critical course feature for nontraditional students
Rhode (2009)	Mixed methods	10 adult students enrolled in professional development certificate program at a private college in NE USA	Educational technology	Computer-mediated communication tools and their effect on perceptions of learning interaction	Activity of blogging valued as superior to instructor-directed asynchronous discussion
Shinkareva and Benson (2007)	Correlation analysis	198 CE professionals taking online course at large Midwestern University, ages 31–45, majority female	Business, teacher education, and library science	Learning ability and competency	Self-regulated learning ability positively correlated with instructional technology competence, self-efficacy, and effort regulation
Sorensen and Murchú (2004)	Theoretical	Graduate students in Denmark and Ireland	Education	Online course design	Using community of inquiry as the online instructional design framework
Stafford and Lindsey (2007)	Quantitative analysis of internet and email usage	63 students: 21 female, 42 male; 51 ages 18–24 and 12 ages 25–34	Informational technology	Differential student motivations for traditional and online education	Older, nontraditional students reported higher self-perceived technical competency and higher satisfaction with online courses

(continued)

Table 2.2 (continued)

Study	Methodology	Sample/site	Subject content	Learning or instructional dimensions	Findings or propositions
Zembylas (2008)	Case study with discourse analysis	22 in-service teachers at the Open University in Cyprus; 17 of 22 female; average age 36	Master's course on multicultural education and social justice pedagogies	Emotions of online adult learner	Qualitative evidence on adult learners' emotional presence during learning interaction, with gender differentiation

References

Adams, T., & Sean Evans, R. (2004). Educating the educators: Outreach to the college of education distance faculty and Native American Students. *Journal of Library Administration, 41*(1/2), 3–18.

Adeoye, B., & Wentling, R. (2007). The relationship between national culture and the usability of an e-learning system. *International Journal on E-Learning, 6*(1), 119–146.

Almanac of Higher Education. (2007a). *6-year graduation rates of 1999–2000 freshmen at 4-year institutions*. Retrieved January 4, 2012 from http://chronicle.com.libproxy.unm.edu/weekly/almanac/2007/nation/0101404.htm.

Almanac of Higher Education. (2007b). *Graduation rates by state of the U.S. population by racial and ethnic group, 2006*. Retrieved January 4, 2012 from http://chronicle.com.libproxy.unm.edu/weekly/almanac/2007/nation/0101602.htm.

Amant, K. S. (2002). Integrating intercultural online learning experiences into the computer classroom. *Technical Communication Quarterly, 11*(3), 289–315.

Anakwe, U. P., Kessler, E. H., & Christensen, E. W. (1999). Distance learning and cultural diversity: Potential users' perspective. *International Journal of Organizational Analysis, 7*(3), 224–243.

Anderson, B., & Simpson, M. (2007). Ethical issues in online education. *Open Learning, 22*(2), 129–138. Retrieved March 29, 2009, doi:10.1080/02680510701306673.

Angiello, R. (2002). Enrollment and success of Hispanic students in online courses (Report 143). New Jersey: Bergen Community College. Retrieved March 31, 2009, from ERIC database.

Anzaldúa, G. (1987). *Borderlands, la frontera: The new Mestiza* (2nd ed.). San Francisco: Aunt Lute Books.

Arias, A. (2000). Agile learning, new media, and technological infusement at a New University: Serving underrepresented students. JSRI occasional paper. East Lansing: Julian Samora Research Institute. Retrieved March 31, 2009, from ERIC database.

Bennett, J. M., & Bennett, M. J. (1994). Multiculturalism and international education: Domestic and international differences. In G. Althen (Ed.), *Learning across cultures* (pp. 145–165). Washington, DC: NAFSA, Association of International Educators.

Benson, R., & Samarawickrema, G. (2007). Teaching in context: Some implications for e-learning design. In R. Oliver, D. Tan, A. Kit, & C. Cheers (Eds.), *ICT: providing choices for learners and learning* (pp. 61–70). Singapore: ASCILITE.

Bentley, J. P. H., Tinney, M. V., & Chia, B. H. (2005). Intercultural internet-based learning: Know your audience and what it values. *Educational Technology Research and Development, 53*(2), 117–127.

Berkshire, S., & Smith, G. (2000). Bridging the great divide: Connecting Alaska native learners and leaders via "High Touch-High Tech" distance learning. National Association of African American Studies & National Association of Hispanic and Latino Studies: 2000 Literature Monograph Series. Retrieved March 31, 2009, from ERIC database.

Bloomberg, L. (2007). Culture and community: Case study of a video-conferenced graduate distance education program. *Journal of Distance Education, 22*(1), 41–58. Retrieved April 29, 2009, from Education Research Complete database.

Branch, R. M. (1997). Educational technology frameworks that facilitate culturally pluralistic instruction. *Educational Technology, 37*(2), 38–41.

Brayboy, B. M. J., & Maughan, E. (2009). Native American knowledges and the story of the bean. *Harvard Educational Review, 79*(1), 1–21.

Buerck, J., Malmstrom, T., & Peppers, E. (2003). Learning environments and learning styles: Non-traditional student enrollment and success in an internet-based versus a lecture-based computer science course. *Learning Environments Research, 6*(2), 137–155.

Cajete, G. (1994). Look to the mountain: An ecology of Native American education. Ashville, NC: Kivaki Press.

Chávez, A. F. (2007). Islands of empowerment: Facilitating multicultural learning communities in college. *International Journal of Teaching and Learning in Higher Education, 19*(3), 274–288.

Chávez, A. F. (2011). Toward a multicultural ecology of teaching and learning: A critical review of theory & research. *Journal of Excellence in College Teaching, 21*(4), 49–74.

Chávez, A. F., & Guido-DiBrito, F. (1999). Racial and ethnic identity and development. In C. Clark & R. Caffarella (Eds.), *An update on adult development theory: New ways of thinking about the life course* (New Directions for Adult and Continuing Education, Vol. 84, pp. 39–48). San Francisco: Jossey-Bass.

Chávez, A. F., Ke, F., & Herrera, F. (2012). Clan, sage, and sky: Indigenous, Hispano, and Mestizo narratives of learning in New Mexico context. *American Educational Research Journal, 49*(4), 775–806.

Chen, R. T., Bennett, S., & Maton, K. (2008). The adaptation of Chinese international students to online flexible learning: two case studies. *Distance Education, 29*(3), 307–323. Retrieved March 29, 2009, doi:10.1080/01587910802395821

Chen, A., Mashhadi, A., Ang, D., & Harkrider, N. (1999). Cultural issues in the design of technology-enhanced learning systems. *British Journal of Educational Technology, 30*(3), 217. Retrieved March 29, 2009, from Education Research Complete database.

Chernish, W., DeFranco, A., Lindner, J., & Dooley, K. (2005). Does it matter? Analyzing the results of three different learning delivery methods. *Quarterly Review of Distance Education, 6*(2), 87–95. Retrieved March 29, 2009, from Education Research Complete database.

Chesler, M., Lewis, A., & Crowfoot, J. (2005). *Challenging racism in higher education: Promoting justice*. Lanham: Rowman & Littlefield Publishers.

Chyung, S. (2007). Age and gender differences in online behavior, self-efficacy, and academic performance. *Quarterly Review of Distance Education, 8*(3), 213–222. Retrieved March 29, 2009, from Education Research Complete database.

Collis, B. (1999). Designing for differences: Cultural issues in the design of WWW-based course-support sites. *British Journal of Educational Technology, 30*(3), 201–215.

Covarrubias, P. O., & Windchief, S. W. (2009). Silences in stewardship: Some American Indian college students' examples. *The Howard Journal of Communications, 20*(4), 333–352.

Crane, R. (2005). Adults, access and e learning. *International Journal of Learning, 12*(5), 211–214. Retrieved March 29, 2009, from Education Research Complete database.

Dahl, J. (2004). How to bring distance Ed to underserved opulations. *Distance Education Report, 8*(21), 5–7. Retrieved March 29, 2009, from Education Research Complete database.

Davis, J. (2006). Designing an online course for nontraditional students: Revisiting the essentials. *International Journal of Learning, 12*(10), 121–127.

de Lange, P., Waldmann, E., & Wyatt, K. (1997). Personal characteristics and academic achievement of undergraduate accounting students studying through open learning. *Accounting Education, 6*(4), 295–306. Retrieved April 29, 2009, doi:10.1080/096392897331370.

Delgado Bernal, D. (2001). Learning and living pedagogies of the home: The Mestiza consciousness of Chicana students. *Qualitative Studies in Education, 14*(5), 623–639.

Dillon, P., Wang, R., & Tearle, P. (2007). Cultural disconnection in virtual education. *Pedagogy, Culture & Society, 15*(2), 153–174. Retrieved March 29, 2009, doi:10.1080/14681360701403565.

Elenes, C. A., Delgado Bernal, D., González, F., Trinidad, R., & Villenas, S. (2000). *Chicana/Mexicana feminist pedagogies: Consejos, respeto, y educacion in everyday life*. Symposium presented at the annual meeting of the American Educational Research Association, New Orleans.

Evans, S., Wang, R., Yeh, T., Anderson, J., Haija, R., McBratney-Owen, P., et al. (2007). Evaluation of distance learning in an introduction to biostatistics class: A case study. *Statistics Education Research Journal, 6*(2), 59–77. Retrieved March 29, 2009, from Education Research Complete database.

Fried, J. (1994). *Shifting paradigms in student affairs: Culture, context, teaching and learning*. Lanham: American College Personnel Association.

Guido-DiBrito, F., & Chávez, A. F. (2003). Understanding the ethnic self: Learning and teaching in a multicultural world. *Journal of Student Affairs, 7*, 11–21.

Gunawardena, C. N., Nolla, A. C., Wilson, P. L., Lopez-Islas, J. R., Ramirez-Angel, N., & Megchun-Alpizar, R. M. (2001). A cross-cultural study of group process and development in online conferences. *Distance Education, 22*(1), 85–121.

Gurin, P., Dey, E., Hurtado, S., & Gurin, G. (2002). Diversity and higher education: Theory and impact on educational outcomes. *Harvard Educational Review, 72*(3), 330–367.

Hedberg, J., & Brown, I. (2002). Understanding cross-cultural meaning through visual media. *Educational Media International, 39*(1), 23–30. Retrieved April 29, 2009, doi:10.1080/09523980210131123.

Heine, S. J., Kitayama, S., Lehman, D. R., Takata, T., Ide, E., Leung, C., et al. (2001). Divergent consequences of success and failure in Japan and North America: An investigation of self-improving motivations and malleable selves. *Journal of Personality and Social Psychology, 81*(4), 599–615.

Henderson, L. (1996). Instructional design of interactive multimedia. *Educational Technology Research and Development, 44*(4), 85–104.

Henning, E. (2003). 'I click, therefore I am (not)': is cognition 'distributed' or is it 'contained' in borderless e-learning programmes? *International Journal of Training & Development, 7*(4), 303–317. Retrieved April 29, 2009, doi:10.1046/j.1360-3736.2003.00188.x.

Hogan, R. (2009). Attitudes of indigenous peoples toward distance learning in the South Pacific: An empirical study. In G. Siemens & C. Fulford (Eds.), *Proceedings of world conference on educational multimedia, hypermedia and telecommunications 2009* (pp. 1064–1072). Chesapeake: AACE.

Hudson, B., Hudson, A., & Steel, J. (2006). Orchestrating interdependence in an international online learning community. *British Journal of Educational Technology, 37*(5), 733–748. Retrieved April 29, 2009, doi:10.1111/j.1467-8535.2006.00552.x.

Hurd, S., & Xiao, J. (2006). Open and distance language learning at the Shantou Radio and TV University, China, and the Open University, United Kingdom: A cross–cultural perspective. *Open Learning, 21*(3), 205–219.

Ibarra, R. (2000). Studying Latinos in a "Virtual" University: Reframing diversity and academic culture change. Occasional Paper No. 68. Latino studies series. East Lansing: Julian Samora Research Institute. Retrieved March 31, 2009, from ERIC database.

Ibarra, R. (2001). *Beyond affirmative action: Reframing the context of higher education.* Madison: University of Wisconsin.

Johari, A. (2005). Intercultural internet-based learning: Know your audience and what it values. *Educational Technology Research and Development, 53*(2), 117–127.

Johns, A. M., & Kelley Sipp, M. (2004). *Diversity in college classrooms: Practices for today's campuses.* Ann Arbor: University of Michigan Press.

Kasworm, C. E., & Pike, G. R. (1994). Adult undergraduate students: Evaluating the appropriateness of a traditional model of academic performance. *Research in Higher Education, 35*(6), 689–710.

Ke, F., Chávez, A. F., & Herrera, F. (2009). *Web based teaching and learning across culture and age.* Paper presented at the annual meeting of the American Educational Research Association, San Diego.

Knight, M., Dixon, I., Norton, N., & Bentley, C. (2004). Extending learning communities: New technologies, multiple literacies, and culture blind pedagogies. *Urban Review, 36*(2), 101–118. Retrieved March 29, 2009, from Education Research Complete database.

Kuenzi, J. J. (2008). *Science, technology, engineering, and mathematics (STEM) education: Background, federal policy, and legislative action.* Congressional Research Service.

Kumar, K., & Bhattacharya, M. (2007). Designing for learning effectiveness across borders in a multicultural context. *Journal of Interactive Learning Research, 18*(1), 111–121. Retrieved April 29, 2009, from Education Research Complete database.

Lauzon, A. (1999). Situating cognition and crossing borders: Resisting the hegemony of mediated education. *British Journal of Educational Technology, 30*(3), 261. Retrieved March 29, 2009, from Education Research Complete database.

Lea, M. (2001). Computer conferencing and assessment: New ways of writing in higher education. *Studies in Higher Education, 26*(2), 163–181.

Lim, D. (2004). Cross cultural differences in online learning motivation. *Educational Media International, 41*(2), 163–173. Retrieved April 29, 2009, doi:10.1080/09523980410001685784.

Lin, C. (2007). e-Learning strategies for aboriginal children in Taiwan. *International Journal of Learning, 14*(6), 153–160. Retrieved April 29, 2009, from Education Research Complete database.

Llambi, L., Margolis, A., Toews, J., Dapueto, J., Esteves, E., Martínez, E., et al. (2008). Distance education for physicians: Adaptation of a Canadian experience to Uruguay. *Journal of Continuing Education in the Health Professions, 28*(2), 79–85. Retrieved April 29, 2009, doi:10.1002/chp.161.

Makoe, M. (2006). South African distance students' accounts of learning in socio-cultural context: A habitus analysis. *Race, Ethnicity & Education, 9*(4), 361–380.

Makoe, M., Richardson, J., & Price, L. (2008). Conceptions of learning in adult students embarking on distance education. *Higher Education, 55*(3), 303–320.

McGivney, V. (2004). Understanding persistence in adult learning. *Open Learning, 19*(1), 33–46.

McLaren, A. (2007). Designing distance instruction for the Arab World. *Distance Learning, 4*(3), 17–21. Retrieved March 29, 2009, from Education Research Complete database.

McLoughlin, C. (1999). Culturally responsive technology use: Developing an on-line community of learners. *British Journal of Educational Technology, 30*(3), 231–243.

McLoughlin, C., & Oliver, R. (2000). Designing learning environments for cultural inclusivity: A case study of Native American online learning at tertiary level. *Australian Journal of Educational Technology, 16*(1), 58–72.

McPatton, M. (2000). The importance of being flexible with assignment deadlines. *Higher Education in Europe, 25*(3), 417–423.

Patton, M. (2000). The importance of being flexible with assignment deadlines. *Higher Education in Europe, 25*(3), 417–423.

Rasmussen, K., Nichols, J., & Ferguson, F. (2006). It's a new world: Multiculturalism in a virtual environment. *Distance Education, 27*(2), 265–278. Retrieved March 29, 2009, doi:10.1080/01587910600789696.

Reeves, T. C. (1992). Evaluating interactive multimedia. *Educational Technology, 32*(5), 47–53.

Reeves, T., & Reeves, P. (1997). Effective dimensions of interactive learning on the world wide web. In B. Khan (Ed.), *Web-based instruction* (pp. 59–66). Englewood Cliffs: Educational Technology Publications.

Rendón, L. I. (2009). *Sentipensante (sensing/thinking) pedagogy: Educating for wholeness, social justice and liberation*. Sterling: Stylus.

Rhode, J. (2009). Interaction equivalency in self-paced online learning environments: An exploration of learner preferences. *International Review of Research in Open & Distance Learning, 10*(1), 1–23.

Rich, A. (1993). Toward a woman centered university. In J. Glazer, E. Bensimon, & B. Townsend (Eds.), *Women in higher education: A feminist perspective* (pp. 121–134). Needham Heights: Ginn Press.

Sanchez, J., Stuckey, M. E., & Morris, R. (1998). Distance learning in Indian country: Becoming the spider on the web. *Journal of American Indian Education, 37*(3), 1–17.

Sang, W. (2007). Cross-cultural delivery of e-learning programmes: Perspectives from Hong Kong. *International Review of Research in Open & Distance Learning, 8*(3), 1–16.

Selinger, M. (2004). Cultural and pedagogical implications of a global e-learning programme. *Cambridge Journal of Education, 34*(2), 223–239.

Shenk, D., Moore, L., & Davis, B. (2004). Teaching an interdisciplinary distance education gerontology course: Benefits of diversity. *Educational Gerontology, 30*(3), 219–235.

Shinkareva, O., & Benson, A. (2007). The relationship between adult students' instructional technology competency and self-directed learning ability in an online course. *Human Resource Development International, 10*(4), 417–435.

Smith, D., & Ayers, D. (2006). Culturally responsive pedagogy and online learning: Implications for the globalized community college. *Community College Journal of Research & Practice, 30*(5/6), 401–415.

Sorensen, E., & Murchú, D. (2004). Designing online learning communities of practice: A democratic perspective. *Journal of Educational Media, 29*(3), 189–200.
Stafford, T., & Lindsey, K. (2007). IP teleconferencing in the wired classroom: Gratifications for distance education. *Journal of Information Systems Education, 18*(2), 227–232.
Stockhausen, L., & Kawashima, A. (2002). The introduction of reflective practice to Japanese nurses. *Reflective Practice, 3*(1), 117–129.
Tisdell, E. (1995). *Creating inclusive adult learning environments: Insights from multicultural education and feminist pedagogy* (Information Series #361). Columbus: Center on Education and Training for Employment. Retrieved from ERIC data base. (ED384827).
Tu, C. (2001). How Chinese perceive social presence: An examination of interaction in online learning environment. *Educational Media International, 38*(1), 45–60.
Van den Branden, J., & Lambert, J. (1999). Cultural issues related to transnational open and distance learning in universities: A European problem? *British Journal of Educational Technology, 30*(3), 251–260.
Venter, K. (2003). Coping with isolation: The role of culture in adult distance learners' use of surrogates. *Open Learning, 18*(3), 271–287.
Viernes Turner, C. S. (1994). Guests in someone else's house: Students of color. *The Review of Higher Education, 17*(4), 355–370.
Villalpando, O., & Solórzano, D. (2005). The role of culture in college preparation programs: A review of the research literature. In Z. B. Corwin, J. Colyar, & W. G. Tierney (Eds.), *Preparing for college: Nine elements of effective outreach* (pp. 13–28). Albany: State University of New York Press.
Wang, M. (2007). Designing online courses that effectively engage learners from diverse cultural backgrounds. *British Journal of Educational Technology, 38*(2), 294–311.
Weinstein, G., & Obear, K. (1992). Bias issues in the classroom: Encounters with the teaching self. *New Directions in Teaching and Learning, 52*, 39–50. San Francisco: Jossey-Bass.
Williams, S. W., Watkins, K., Daley, B., Courtenay, B., Davis, M., & Dymock, D. (2001). Facilitating cross-cultural online discussion groups: Implications for practice. *Distance Education, 22*(1), 151–167.
Wu, B., & Teoh, P. A. (2008). A comparative analysis of learners interaction in the online learning management systems: Does national culture matter? *Asian Association of Open Universities Journal, 3*(1), 1–16.
Yildiz, S., & Bichelmeyer, B. A. (2003). Exploring electronic forum participation and interaction by EFL speakers in two web-based graduate-level courses. *Distance Education, 24*(2), 175–193.
Yong, Y., & Parrella, A. (2004). Towards accommodating learning diversity in online education. In *Online classroom* (pp. 4–5). Madison, WI: Magna Publications.
Zembylas, M. (2008). Adult learners' emotions in online learning. *Distance Education, 29*(1), 71–87.
Zepke, N., & Leach, L. (2002). Appropriate pedagogy and technology in a cross-cultural distance education context. *Teaching in Higher Education, 7*(3), 309–321.

Chapter 3
A Two-Year Research Project on Web-Based Teaching and Learning

During the academic years 2008–2010, a 2-year in situ study was conducted on web-based teaching and learning at a major research university in the southwest United States. We utilized a variety of qualitative and quantitative techniques to explore the impact of online pedagogies and contexts on the learning experiences of a diversity of college students living in rural and urban areas, with an emphasis on learners of nontraditional age and/or minority status. The study primarily addressed three research questions:

- To what extent are online learning and interaction experiences and performances consistent across varied ethnic and age groups and in what ways do they vary?
- What online instructional contexts do students and faculty identify as supporting learning and student success, especially for nontraditional and minority students?
- What are the relationships between online instructional contexts, online learning interaction performance, and perceived learning success of students with diverse ethnicity/culture and age background?

Research Design

For this study we used concurrent transformative design (Creswell, Plano Clark, Gutmann, & Hanson, 2003), encompassing qualitative case study research and quantitative causal-comparative research. Data was collected over two school years via surveys, iterative interviews, quantified content analysis (with online discussion transcripts), and document and artifact analysis (with course documents and learning activity logs).

F. Ke and A.F. Chávez, *Web-Based Teaching and Learning across Culture and Age*,
DOI 10.1007/978-1-4614-0863-5_3,

Sites and Participants

A major university and its 4 branch campuses in a southwestern state were chosen for this study. Like other states, colleges in this state utilize web-based learning systems to supplement campus-based learning. Web-based learning courses are often chosen by students with challenging life circumstances. Many are Native and Hispanic American students who manage cultural, familial, geographic, and economic circumstances that often make traditional collegiate environments unrealistic. Adult students enrolled in online courses often remain "place-bound" because of tribal and/or extended family responsibilities or are time constrained because of job availability. During the time of the study, WebCT was the distance-based learning system in place.

Serving 32,914 on its main campus, the university also provides instruction to 10,000 students via various branch campuses and web-based distance course offerings in remote parts of the state. The university is distinctive as a Hispanic serving institution. The university has a minority and international student population of approximately 54.2 % (37.0 % Hispanic, 5.5 % Native American, 8.1 % other American minority ethnic groups, and 3.6 % international). One of the branch community campuses enrolls 77 % or 2,223 Native American students, the largest population of Native American students of any college in the USA. Students of this university are primarily commuters who also work 30 or more hours per week, with only 1,500 students living on campus.

Multilevel sampling was used for the qualitative and quantitative components of the study. Participant recruiting lasted through the two school years. Students were recruited from 36 undergraduate and graduate online courses from academic disciplines in education, nursing, business, engineering, natural science, social sciences, and humanities. These courses were purposely selected based on the following criteria: (a) offered online via the web-based learning management system (e.g., WebCT); (b) having a diverse student body in terms of ethnic status and age, with nontraditional and minority students comprising 30 % or more of the student enrollment; (c) involving online interactions, such as discussions, in learning activities; (d) differing in instructional strategies (e.g., task design, information delivery, and learning support); and online interaction contexts (e.g., different levels of presence and facilitation by the instructor, different online discussion tasks). From the recruited participants, a smaller sample was purposefully selected for individual interviewing. Participants were selected to represent diverse age, ethnic status, gender, prior online learning/teaching experiences, and educational backgrounds.

Student participants enrolled in these courses ranged in ages between 18 and 64, with 32.6 as the mean. Minority students made up around 46 % of participants including Latino/Hispanic American (27 %), Native American (9 %), and a small number of Asian American (3 %), African American (3 %), as well as international students (4 %). It should be noted that in this project a single student could be enrolled in multiple sampled courses. With each course, this student's learning activity and survey data were collected as the data for a single subject. Overall, data of 463 subjects were collected.

Data Collection and Analysis

Qualitative data were collected from interviewing, online observation of the instructional/learning events, content analysis of online discussion transcripts, and artifact analyses of course documents. Data from different resources were corroborated with each other, and the analysis of qualitative data generally included three stages: (1) thematic analysis (axial) focused on systematically extracting emergent patterns and themes of teaching strategies, learning participation, intergenerational interactions, cross-cultural interactions, and the mediation role of technologies; (2) coding (coaxial) deepened the systematic analysis through an applied sorting of data into categories derived from the axial stage; and (3) data transformation (Onwuegbuzie & Teddlie, 2003). Peer debriefing and member checking were part of data collection (Lincoln & Guba, 1985). Peer debriefing consisted of formal reviews of data among the coders of the study data and informal reviews with a group of education graduate students. Member checks were conducted informally with participating instructors and students during the interview process. We restated and shared the reported information and/or observed notes and then questioned the participants to determine accuracy or provide alternative interpretations.

Interviewing

Following semi-structured interviewing protocols, a selected sample of online instructors and students were individually interviewed on their teaching and learning experiences and perceptions, with a focus on their teaching or learning philosophy and planning, online facilitation or interaction experiences, ways of instruction delivery or learning participation, and teaching or learning perceptions. The student interviews were conducted either face-to-face or by phone, pending on interviewees' choices. Instructor interviews were conducted face-to-face. The interviews with participants were conducted iteratively during the midterm and the end of school semesters. Each interview lasted 45–60 min.

We employed a qualitative thematic analysis (Miles & Huberman, 1994) with interview transcripts to examine recurring themes on course instruction and interaction contexts, as well as learning and interaction processes from participants' perspective. These qualitative themes were then compared and congregated with the findings of discourse and artifact analysis.

Online Observation of Learning Events

We conducted online observations of synchronous web conferencing and text-chat sessions of a selected sample of online courses representing different academic disciplines and instructional contexts. Observations were open and descriptive in nature, while focusing on understanding when, how, why, and with whom an online instructional event and/or learning interaction occurred. Conversations and actions of online instructors and students throughout the sessions were archived. Additionally, online observations were recorded by field notes on a weekly basis. We then conducted *categorical aggregation analysis* (i.e., categorizing the critical properties of meaningful actions or instances and classifying them into aggregations, Stake, 1995) with the observed activities to examine key patterns of online learning/interaction processes, such as their purpose, content, and typical characteristics. To gain a deep sense of online learning and interaction, we first coded the data into reasonable, meaningful units that signify categories and subcategories of the online learning processes (Creswell, 2007). Via a systematic coding method (Marshall & Rossman, 2006), we then reduced and summarized the coded data based on categories emerging from the data. The analysis of learning events contributed an initial taxonomy of categories which was then refined and extended via a constant comparison, pattern matching, and frequency coding.

Online Discussion Transcripts

Transcripts of online class discussions of each course throughout the entire school semester were exported from WebCT along with all meta-information (e.g., time stamps). For analysis, 6 weeks of discussion transcripts were gathered and coded for each course (two at the second and third school week, two at the midterm, and two at the end of the school term). The sample time frames were selected to represent the beginning, middle, and end phases of a course and enable an overtime analysis of online discussions occurring during a school semester. Compelling findings from online documents and virtual observations stimulated new questions for interviewing.

In this study, discourse analysis of the online discussion transcripts included two dimensions – epistemic and participation. For the epistemic dimension, we focused on the content of students' contribution by analyzing the purpose of contribution, evidence of knowledge building, and the expression of identity. For the participation dimension, we examined the quantity of students' participation and contribution, including the number of initiated posts, responses, and reciprocal replies. We also explored the potential heterogeneity of participation among students by conducting a cross-case analysis with students of diverse characteristics.

In this study we utilized an online interaction analysis scheme that integrates sociocultural and social constructivist perspectives on *individual cognition* and *collective development* within students' online interactions (Gee & Green, 1998). Specifically, *Online Learning Interaction Model* (OLIM, Ke & Xie, 2009) is a synthesis of two representative content analysis schemes in the distance education literature: Henri's work (1992), which examines the quality of online postings with a focus on individual conceptual growth or cognition situated in dialogues, and the framework of Gunawardena, Constance, and Anderson (1997), which mainly examines evidence of collective knowledge development in an open-ended online debate forum. The OLIM has been field-tested and refined in the current study (Ke, 2010;

Ke & Xie, 2009). The unit of interaction analysis was *thematic unit* or *unit of meaning* (Henri, 1992). The analysis focused on a consistent theme or idea that was associated with a syntactic unit (i.e., an online discussion post in this study) (Rourke, Anderson, Garrison, & Archer, 1999). Each unit was classified into one of the eight analytic categories of online interaction purpose/content. The coding framework is outlined in Table 3.1.

Coding Process: Three raters coded the online discussion transcripts. After reaching 100 % agreement on coding two sample weeks' transcripts, all raters double-blindly coded the remaining transcripts. The average inter-rater reliability is .92. The three raters also discussed differences in their codes and reached an agreement at 100 %. The final revised codes were used for later analyses.

Document or Artifact Analysis of Online Course Documents

An artifact analysis was conducted with online course documents to generate a description of online interaction contexts. To develop a *thick description* (Lincoln & Guba, 1985) and gain a deep sense of online courses as learning environments, we first utilized thematic analysis (Miles & Huberman, 1994) to categorize the design elements of the sampled online course sites and students' discussion experiences. Second, we followed a systematic coding method (Marshall & Rossman, 2006) to analyze and reduce data according to the themes found and searched for outlying and subtle themes. The patterns or categories of the instructional and interaction contexts of online courses have emerged from the artifact analysis and will be described in Chaps. 4 and 6.

Quantitative Data and Analyses

Quantitative data were collected from surveys and student learning activity logs. Quantitative surveys were developed and used to measure participants' perceptions of online instructional strategies, learning environment climate, learning satisfaction, and perceived achievements. These surveys also included open-ended questions that were converted into narrative data and analyzed qualitatively.

At the end of the semester, a learning experience survey was distributed to all participating online students. This survey was developed based on the *Distance Education Learning Environments Survey* (DELES, Walker & Fraser, 2005) and *Motivated Strategies for Learning Questionnaire* (MSLQ, Pintrich & De Groot, 1990). The DELES was developed to measure learners' perceptions of an online course environment and validated through the use of both graduate-level and undergraduate students from 13 countries, primarily the United States, Australia, New Zealand, and Canada. The alpha reliability coefficient of the 7 scales of the survey ranged from .75 to .95 (Walker & Fraser, 2005). The survey contained 42, 5-point Likert-scaled items in seven scales. The first six scales evaluated the

Table 3.1 Coding framework for online interactions (Ke, 2010; Ke & Xie, 2009)

Code	Category		Definition & examples
S	Social interaction		• Having the indicators of greetings, giving credit, deciding (e.g., "I agree with you"), and emotional expressions • Sharing personal life experiences that do not contribute to knowledge sharing or construction
K1	Knowledge sharing & construction	Knowledge sharing: • Information • Idea • Question	 • Sharing facts or information without interpretation or evaluation • Sharing opinions without elaboration or explanation • Fact-seeking or clarification question
K2		Egocentric elaboration: • Information • Idea	 • Elaborating one's own arguments/concepts/problem solutions, citing one's own experience/observation (e.g., "From my experiences…", "I remember when I was in physics…") or citing books, reading materials, and knowledge learned before (e.g., "As the book says…", "According to X theory…");
K3		Allocentric elaboration: • Information • Idea • Question	Interpreting and evaluating peers' perspectives with elaboration, including: • Interpreting and/or evaluation: e.g., "I agree with you… because", "I have to disagree with Karen…due to", "Let me take this a step further" • Alternative-view-seeking or explanation-seeking question: e.g., "Most of you have only discussed positive aspects, I want to know if you have had negative experiences"
K4		Knowledge creation: • Information • Idea	 • Synthesis • Rise-above • Application: planning application of new knowledge
M1	Management	Environment management	Questioning and clarification on: • Technological environment • Course requirement e.g., "Anyone knows how to quote a message?"
M2		Coordination	Planning and coordination of collaborative projects and inquiries e.g., "Tom, can you do task 1 and I will do task 2?"
M3		Reflection & self-regulation	Reflection and self-evaluation on interaction, project, and other learning processes: e.g., "I could have use X to help me to learn."

constructs of *instructor-student interaction, student interaction, personal relevance, authentic learning, active learning,* and *student autonomy*, and the last scale evaluated learners' overall satisfaction with web-based distance education (all $\alpha > .90$). The MSLQ assesses college students' motivational orientations and their use of different cognitive and metacognitive learning strategies for a college course. MSLQ has been validated in prior studies, with its component scales designed to be modular, used together or singly to fit the needs of the researcher (Pintrich & De Groot, 1990). In this project, a shortened version of MSLQ was used, comprising 25 seven-point items in three component scales. The first scale measured goal orientation, including extrinsic motivation (2-item, $\alpha = .65$) and intrinsic motivation (2-item, $\alpha = .65$). The second scale measured cognitive and metacognitive strategies, including the constructs of elaboration (4-item, $\alpha = .75$), organization (2-item, $\alpha = .64$), critical thinking (3-item, $\alpha = .74$), and metacognitive self-regulation (5-item, $\alpha = .67$). The third scale measured resource management (7-item, $\alpha = .63$), including that for time and study environment, effort regulation, and help seeking.

Students in this study also received a short questionnaire that measured their self-perceived computer competence (6-item, 5-point scaled, $\alpha = .97$), satisfaction of the specific online course(s) in which they were enrolled (4-item, 5-point scaled, $\alpha = .96$), time spent on diverse online activities (5 open-ended questions), and comments on learning experiences and perceived learning success (5 open-ended questions).

Participating students' online learning activity logs were exported from the WebCT learning management system into data sheets. For each student, these activity logs recorded the following meta-information: (1) frequency, timing, and duration of accessing the online course site; (2) frequency and duration of interactions with different course learning tools (e.g., email, discussion forum, calendar, chat) and specific actions performed (e.g., read, send, or post a message); and (3) frequency and duration of using diverse learning materials or objects (e.g., assessments, assignments, web links, content files, and media library).

Adopting a causal-comparative approach, we then:

- Ran descriptive statistics on the profiles of online participation, intergenerational interaction, cross-cultural interaction, and online learning technology usage among students across different culture and age groups
- Conducted a comparative analysis of nontraditional, minority students and others' online learning participation; perceptions of learning environment climate; involvement with intergenerational and cross-cultural interactions; and perceptions of online learning contexts
- Conducted inferential statistics to predict causal-effect relationships between learner characteristics, specific online instructional strategies, online interaction patterns, and cognitive and affective learning processes and outcomes

Finally, findings from qualitative and quantitative analyses were consolidated and integrated and then reported in the form of statistical data, thematic patterns, and narrative descriptions to address the research questions.

A Summary of Major Findings

This mixed-method, longitudinal study contributed a list of interesting findings. These findings are summarized in the following section and will be described and discussed in Chaps. 4, 5, 6, 7, 8 and 9:

1. Minority status did not predict students' online learning interaction performance and perceived learning success within a specific online course. However, it did predict students' attitudes toward online distance education in general, with minority students (e.g., Hispanic and Navajo) being less confident and comfortable about taking courses online. It also predicted students' satisfaction with the student-to-instructor interaction, with minority students reporting more favorable perception of the student-to-instructor interaction.
2. The older, the better: Older adult students tended to perform more collaborative and deep-learning-oriented online interactions, demonstrated higher time commitment for online and offline learning activities, and self-reported a greater sense of learning success.
3. Students' cultural and age-related identity was present in their online discussions, and there was a significant effect of cultural cues within a post in eliciting peer replies. Correspondingly, cross-cultural and intergenerational interactions were generally considered valuable to learning experiences. However, cross-cultural adaption and forbearance were also frequently reported and observed during online interactions.
4. A conceptual framework depicting valuable online instructional contexts emerged from the data comprising the online courses' sites/materials, online discussion transcripts, and interviews/surveys of online instructors/students.
5. A model of online interaction transcript analysis – *Online Interaction Model* – was developed based on the theoretical framework of *deep* learning (Cercone, 2008; Fink, 2003) and a synthesis of representative content analysis schemes in the distance education literature (Gunawardena, Lowe, & Anderson, 1997; Henri, 1992). The model got infield investigated and refined through this current study.
6. A model of eight *cultural constructs in teaching and learning* was conceptualized through anthropological theory and developed further based on interview and course site analysis. Findings suggest that Native and Hispanic American students learn best from a very different epistemology and practice than Caucasian Northern European American students within each of the eight constructs.
7. Native American students in this study were distinctive from other students in their conscious identification of specific pedagogical factors helpful to their learning in web-based courses specifically including benefitting from the visual and interactive nature of online courses, historical archival access to all course materials throughout the semester, learning by "doing online," and reflection time usually made possible by the nature of online learning.

8. The data from online instructional and interaction contexts across multiple academic disciplines indicated that a course with a balanced and inclusive design of all three interaction modes (student-to-student, student-to-content, and student-to-teacher) promoted online students' knowledge construction and reflective learning most. This finding contributed a valuable infield examination of the *equivalency theory* of online interactions by Anderson (2003). The finding did not support Anderson's design proposition that an online instructional designer can substitute one type of interaction for one of the others with little loss in educational effectiveness. Study findings also suggest that a course that prioritized student-to-student interactions reinforced knowledge-constructive online discussions. There was a disciplinary effect on the interactivity and amount of social and knowledge-sharing discussions, with online courses of an *applied* academic discipline (Neumann, Parry, & Becher, 2002) associated with more social and knowledge-sharing discussions.
9. Using structural equation modeling (SEM), we developed and verified hypothesized models on the relationships between perceived online learning environment climate, motivated strategies for learning, and perceived learning success of students with diverse ethnicity/culture and age backgrounds.
10. By consolidating the aforementioned findings, we proposed a data-driven online instructional design model that can work as a field guide on cross-cultural and intergenerational teaching and learning for online education practitioners.

References

Anderson, T. (2003). Modes of interaction in distance education: Recent developments and research questions. In M. Moore (Ed.), *Handbook of distance education* (pp. 129–144). Mahwah: Lawrence Erlbaum.

Cercone, K. (2008). Characteristics of adult learners with implications for online learning design. *AACE Journal, 16*(2), 137–159.

Creswell, J. W. (2007). *Qualitative inquiry and research design: Choosing among five approaches.* Thousand Oaks: Sage.

Creswell, J. W, Plano Clark, V. L., Guttmann, M. L., & Hanson, E. E. (2003). Advanced mixed methods research design. In A.Tashakkori & C. Teddlie (Eds.), *Handbook of mixed methods in social and behavioral research* (pp. 209–240). Thousand Oaks, CA: Sage.

Fink, L. D. (2003). *Creating significant learning experiences: An integrated approach to designing college courses.* San Francisco: Jossey Bass.

Gee, J. P., & Green, J. L. (1998). Discourse analysis, learning, and social practice: A methodological study. *Review of Research in Education, 23*, 119–169.

Gunawardena, C. N., Constance, A. L., & Anderson, T. (1997). Analysis of a global online debate and the development of an interaction analysis model examining social construction of knowledge in computer conferencing. *Journal of Educational Computing Research, 17*(4), 397–431.

Gunawardena, C. N., Lowe, C. A., & Anderson, T. (1997). Analysis of a global online debate and the development of an interaction analysis model for examining social construction of knowledge in computer conferencing. *Journal of Educational Computing Research, 17*(4), 395–429.

Henri, F. (1992). Computer conferencing and content analysis. In A. R. Kaye (Ed.), *Collaborative learning through computer conferencing: The Najaden papers* (pp. 117–136). Berlin: Springer.
Ke, F. (2010). Examining online teaching, cognitive, and social presence for adult students. *Computers in Education, 55*(2), 808–820.
Ke, F., & Xie, K. (2009). Toward deep learning for adult students in online courses. *The Internet and Higher Education, 12*(3–4), 136–145.
Lincoln, Y. S., & Guba, E. G. (1985). *Naturalistic inquiry*. Beverly Hills: Sage.
Marshall, C., & Rossman, G. B. (2006). *Designing qualitative research*. Newbury Park: Sage.
Miles, M. B., & Huberman, A. M. (1994). *Qualitative data analysis: An expanded sourcebook*. Thousand Oaks: Sage.
Neumann, R., Parry, S., & Becher, T. (2002). Teaching and learning in their disciplinary contexts: A conceptual analysis. *Studies in Higher Education, 27*(4), 405–418.
Onwuegbuzie, A. J., & Teddlie, C. (2003). A framework for analyzing data in mixed methods research. In A. Tashakkori & C. Teddlie (Eds.), *Handbook of mixed methods in social and behavioral research* (pp. 351–383). Thousand Oaks: Sage.
Pintrich, P. R., & De Groot, E. V. (1990). Motivational and self-regulated learning components of classroom academic performance. *Journal of Educational Psychology, 82*(1), 33–40.
Rourke, L., Anderson, T., Garrison, D. R., & Archer, W. (1999). Assessing social presence in asynchronous text-based computer. *Journal of Distance Education, 14*(2), 50–71.
Stake, R. E. (1995). *The art of case study research*. Thousand Oaks: Sage.
Walker, S. L., & Fraser, B. J. (2005). Development and validation of an instrument for assessing distance education learning environments in higher education: The Distance Education Learning Environments Survey (DELES). *Learning Environments Research, 8*(3), 289–308.

Part II
Study Findings

Chapter 4
Diversity in Online Learning Interaction and Participation

In this chapter, the nature of online learning is depicted using the theoretical construct of *interaction*. Interaction is viewed as a core part of the educational experience, because "interaction between students, teachers, and content is presumed to play in all of formal education" (Bernard et al., 2009, p. 1246). It is also examined as a core indicator for deep learning in previous studies (e.g., Garrison & Cleveland-Innes, 2005; Ke & Xie, 2009; Offir, Lev, & Bezalel, 2008; Osman & Herring, 2007). According to social constructivism, knowledge is constructed by negotiation of meaning that emerges through interaction and collaboration of learners and by learners' active experience of or interaction with the environment (Vygotsky, 1978). Thus, online interaction is both a process that composes learning experiences and an outcome resulting from learners' engagement with the learning environment (Garrison & Cleveland-Innes, 2005). The literature on web-based education indicates that online learners interact with course content, other learners, the instructor, and the technological medium used in the course (Thurmond & Wambach, 2004). Interactions for learning are both asymmetrical (i.e., student-to-content) and symmetrical communication (i.e., student-to-student and student-to-instructor) (Anderson, 2003; Moore, 1989) and are mediated by technological and pedagogical contexts in an online learning setting.

In this chapter, we focus on describing our research findings on cultural and age-related diversity in online learners' performance and perceptions of student-student, student-instructor, and student-content interactions. These findings emerged from the data collected through a learning experience survey, interviewing, content analysis of online discussion transcripts, and analysis of online learning activity log files over two academic years. They highlight the role of technology-mediated learning interactions in framing learning and success for learners across cultures and intergenerational learners.

F. Ke and A.F. Chávez, *Web-Based Teaching and Learning across Culture and Age*,
DOI 10.1007/978-1-4614-0863-5_4,

Student-Student Interactions

Quantity and Quality of Online Discussions

Group comparison of online discussion participation and performance between Caucasian students and students of minority groups in the sampled courses did not indicate a significant difference. The t-tests on the quantity of online discussion posts that students initiated and responded, including those on the quantity of online discussion threads in which students participated, did not indicate a significant difference between Caucasian and minority students ($p > .05$). Numerically, Caucasian students appeared to elicit more replies ($M = 9.32$, SD = 8.68) than students of minority ethnicities ($M = 6.57$, SD = 6.32) and had more posts replied ($M = 7.94$, SD = 8.55) than minority students ($M = 5.43$, SD = 4.88). This difference, however, was not statistically significant. It should be noted that students of the Caucasian group had a significantly higher mean in age ($M = 34.92$, SD = 12.18) than those of other groups, $F\ (5, 379) = 4.21$, $p = .001$.

The correlation analysis between age and online discussion participation based on the learning activity log files indicated a significant association between the online learner's age and messages posted, $r = .24$, $p = .003$, $n = 392$. Older learners tended to post more online discussion messages.

The learning experience survey results did not indicate a significant role of ethnic status on learners' participation in student-student interaction either. Specifically, there is no ethnicity-related diversity in self-reported time spent in online discussion posting and reading, or perceived peer-interaction participation. On the other hand, there was a significant association between age and self-reported time spent in online discussion posting ($r = .14$, $p = .006$, $n = 392$), between age and reading ($r = .14$, $p = .007$, $n = 392$), and between age and perceived peer-interaction participation ($r = .20$, $p < .001$, $n = 392$). In particular, older learners tended to report more time spent in online discussion participation and higher levels of peer-interaction participation.

Content analysis of online discussion transcripts did not indicate a significant ethnicity-oriented cultural difference or age-related diversity in the content and knowledge presence of online discussion posts. The sampled online discussion posts were broken down into thematic units and coded via the *Online Interaction Model* (Ke, 2010; presented via Table 3.1 in Chap. 3). Overall, around 16 % of the thematic units contained social interactions. Around 76 % of the thematic units conveyed knowledge sharing and construction (e.g., information sharing, elaboration, and knowledge synthesis). Around 10 % of thematic units also reflected the interaction for *learning management* (e.g., inquiries on course requirement and technical interface, project coordination, and self-reflection and regulation). This finding indicated that online students in general engaged in interactions for the purpose of knowledge sharing and construction, with less effort contributed to interactions for social or learning management purposes. On the other hand, online students contributed less online discussions that synthesize peer students' perspectives or online posts to achieve higher planes of understanding or knowledge building (coded as K4 in Table 3.1, with only 2 %), or discussions indicative of self-reflection about the learning process (coded as M3 in Table 3.1, with only 1 %).

Diversity in Experience and Perception of Student-Student Interaction

In the learning experience survey, around 64 % of student participants agreed or strongly agreed that they actively participated in peer-interaction activities, such as information sharing, idea discussion, peer review, and collaborative work. Around 71 % of students self-reported satisfaction with the peer interaction occurring in their online classes. Interestingly, around 15 % of students reported satisfaction with low-level peer interaction (i.e., "the less the better"). Those students expressed preference for an independent ("loner") style of learning and reported peer interaction as optional for learning success: "I am easily distracted when other students are involved in my studies" or "I work pretty independently if I can and would only reach out if I needed to." Around 29 % of students reported dissatisfaction with peer interactions in their online courses, with 22 % complaining about the lack of quantity or quality in the online peer interaction, 3 % complaining about the overwhelming nature of online discussions, and another 4 % expressing dislike of the online interaction environment or dissatisfaction with their classmates' interaction performance.

Such a diversity in perceptions of peer interaction, based on correlation analyses, was not significantly associated with students' cultural or age status. Rather, the diversity in learners' perspectives of peer interaction reflects the diversity in their customs of online learning participation. Their online learning customs, as interview and survey responses indicated, emerged from the following: (a) diverse conceptions and interpretations about online interaction participation, (b) disciplinary- or subject-content-confined learning participation customs, and (c) interaction participation nurtured by instructional design practices.

Diverse Interpretations of Interaction Participation

We observed that students expected different learning experiences from an online class. Online learners who seemed to equate online learning with independent study reported peer interaction as unexpected and unwanted: "I don't care for the student-to-student interaction. If I wanted that, I would take a classroom course. I'd rather focus on the subject and learn straight from the instructor." Other students reported peer interaction as a valuable form of learner support that broadened their knowledge base by getting them to "read about the experiences," helped them refine comprehension and understanding by "bouncing ideas off of other students, gaining valuable insight from others," and enabled peer benchmarking "to ensure that we are all on the same page."

Even among students who embraced online peer interaction, there were different interpretations of "adequate" interactions. Some were grade-driven, while others pursued "spontaneous" interaction. During interviewing, most nontraditional students – usually full-time employees who juggle school, work, family, and/or community commitments – reported the pattern of "catching the deadline" throughout an academic semester. Such a pattern is exemplified by the following interview quotation:

> Well, I work in my own home and I work from home. And so depending on whenever my daughter takes her nap, I tell myself well, if my daughter's gonna be taking a nap for two hours. I've gotta get online and do this and do that. And when my husband comes home after work, he has his time with her. So when he's doing that with her, I'm online. So I'm probably online six or seven hours a day. So, like referring back to the syllabus, or am I getting the requirements due? I gotta check my calendar. Has anyone e-mailed me? I gotta do my posts. I need to do video; I need to respond on my journal. My calendar book is shaded in three different colors for three different classes. I start from the top and then I work my way down to the bottom. I have a calendar that sits by my right side every day. And then on Sunday night, I'll sit here through a whole week and say, okay, journal on Tuesday 508, journal on Wednesday 593. I gotta write this two-page paper. I gotta do my response paper, my activities. And I write it all out for the week. Like I said, all my modules are highlighted for how long I knew the module is. And every day that I need to post I'll write on that specific module color, post, post, post. That way when I get to Wednesday, it says post 508 (the number of the online course), I'll post on my 508 and then I'll cross it off. (participant Mary)

The alignment of the learning schedule with a tight life schedule is obvious in the above quotation. Like Mary, most student participants reported that they "have a routine and a schedule" of online learning participation. They preferred to get an explicit guideline informing the expected online learning participation, especially that for peer interaction – when posts are due, what is expected for the amount and the timing of the initial post and response, with a rubric "telling me exactly what it is I need to write." Their preference for "clarity" was usually a consequence of the prevalence of multitasking in their life and could lead to grade-related peer-interaction participation. As a participant put, "Whenever I do go to these online discussions is whenever the professor asks us to." At the same time, student participants generally voiced a dislike for "posting only because it's part of our expectation" and a desire for "spontaneous" discussions in which "people bring in their issues from their life and bounce ideas off each other."

Another set of conflicting expectations on peer interaction, especially among nontraditional students, was that they appraised the freedom to participate in discussions at a flexible level or timing, but at the same time expressed the need for fair participation or similar online-post contribution among peers. Many student participants reported a disappointment with peers who contributed minimally or way too late and hence "hampered learning."

During the survey and interviewing, student participants frequently complained about social "chit-chat" interaction and characterized it as "aimless." Yet they also reported the lack of online presence of "the personality" and the need for "interfacing with peers" during online interactions, "I know how they are in writing, but I don't get a feel for them. It's kind of hard to remember who's who or whose response you're reading. I don't have any sort of personality for them." The need to "relate to" others seemed to be a prerequisite for forming a sense of bond or trust with an online course community, particularly for students with Hispanic or Native American origins. Such an observation was highlighted by this quotation, "You almost feel more obligated when you're thinking of this human being as a human being versus writing something to somebody… I don't have a trust level with them, I don't know what to expect. If they had a team project for this class, for me, it would be disaster. I just would quit."

Disciplinary Effect

The discussion transcript analysis indicated a significant effect of academic disciplines on the interactivity and content of online discussions. Peer discussions in online courses of an *applied* discipline (i.e., a discipline intrinsically involves real-world problem solving, Neumann, Parry, & Becher, 2002), in comparison with those of a *pure*/basic discipline, were significantly more interactive and involved more online posts for information sharing and social interaction (Ke, 2013).

Such a disciplinary difference, as the interview and survey responses indicated, related to different interpretations on the role of peer interaction in learning (i.e., peer interaction as a disturbance, as an optional support, versus as an essential component of meaningful learning). Students from a *pure* and a *hard* academic discipline (i.e., a discipline involving agreed ordering of knowledge, such as natural science and statistics; Neumann et al., 2002) usually viewed online learning as an independent, correspondence-education-like experience and hence tended to describe peer interaction as "forced and aimless" or an optional support. In comparison, students from an applied discipline or a soft discipline (e.g., nursing, education, business) valued collaborative inquiry and enjoyed the knowledge construction process that occurred via "sharing experiences and insights." It is difficult to determine from our study the factors influencing these discipline-related, differing perspectives. Some possibilities include the norms and culture of specific academic disciplines, personality and other aspects of individual type that are attracted to specific disciplines, and the direct application possibilities of some disciplines versus more abstract nature of others.

Mediation of Instructional Design

Online students' interaction participation was mediated by various instructional design practices. In particular, an authentic, inquiry-based peer-interaction task was found to be critical to motivate proactive performance of knowledge-constructive interaction. For example, both instructor and student participants concurred that the arrangement of real-life scenarios or cases that call for the sharing of hands-on problem-solving experiences, in comparison with a close-ended discussion on a drill question or a comprehension-based discussion on the reading, motivated more "thoughtful discussion with the material, instead of *regurgitating* the material." They also praised a balanced usage of small group- and class-wide online discussions. For example, an instructor participant, with seven years of online teaching experience, explained why she chose to let students interact in groups more than with the whole class:

> I did that (group discussion forum) at the request of the students. I had also asked the students if they had a preference whether they (group discussion forums) were open or closed. Oftentimes students feel overwhelmed when they log onto the web and they see 900 postings or whatever the number is. The second piece that I have found (about the group discussion

> forum) is even though there are various possibilities in how the discussions go, typically the discussions are very similar from group to group, and there is not anything major or drastically different going on in a different group. And so what they actually pick up and benefit from by feeling obligated to go read the discussion postings on another group probably has minimal benefit. And then you have to outweigh the benefits and the stresses. But again I let the students have voice to that. And I think of the students. I only had two out of 23 that said they would like to read all of the other postings.

Aside from graded group discussions, this instructor had also set up a few non-graded online discussion tasks that were open to the entire class in order to serve learners "who really felt like they benefit a lot from the discussion." Such a practice was echoed by other interviewed instructors, who observed that the high quality or the richness of an online discussion was usually associated with the discussion participants who were interested in what they were doing, rather than those who "were only jumping through a hoop to get a grade."

Another online instructional element that enhanced students' participation in discussion was instructor's feedback. By giving individualized comments and probes, an online instructor can foster the presence of individualized attention in the online learning setting. Getting individualized instructor feedback during online discussions, citing a student participant, would feel like the instructor *is making eye contact* with the student.

Nurturing virtual leadership and enabling spontaneous multimodal interactions were another two design practices frequently reported as reinforcing peer interaction. Certain examined courses explicitly required students to lead or facilitate different discussion forums. For example, peer discussion leaders were assigned responsibility to design the initiating post or inquiry question based on the readings and then act as the discussant in the discussion forum. Besides online discussion forums, web conferencing (that afforded both video and audio communication via a video conferencing tool such as Elluminate or Webex) and text chat (that worked well with the feature of "online status" to enable a spontaneous interaction among online students) was quickly embraced and widely used by online instructors and students. As an alternative to asynchronous, text-based online discussion, these communication tools afforded simultaneous, spontaneous ('interact when you need'), and multimodal interactions and hence more effectively served learners who preferred high-context, personable, and/or nonverbal communication, or were "talkers more than writers."

Technology-Mediated Peer Interaction for Diverse Learners

The affordance of online interaction technologies, especially online discussion forums, mediated the processes of information sharing, processing, assimilation, and/or accommodation among diverse learners, leading to diverse perspectives on the advantages/disadvantages of technology-mediated online interaction.

Weighted Down or Digest

Many student participants deemed the text-tense, asynchronous discussion forum as a "weighted-down" way of communication. The following quotations explicated their perceptions:

> Again, I think some people are obviously better learners at reading and interpreting text. I'm not one of those.
>
> Communicating in writing adds a specific set of rules and connotations because people are prone to misunderstanding more so, and then it takes time to clear it up. So, in that sense it's kind of hard. It's like trying to drag a lot of weight as you walk. It just feels hard sometimes. And it's not the concept of the course itself, but the way of the communication is weighted down. Because I think everyone in the class does enjoy flexibility. They're also people who travel a lot, so they do like the fact that it's – we're not bound by a certain place. We do pay a price for that in that communication is slower and cumbersome, and these people get busy and don't post or don't reply; then it's sort of held up. I think since it's a graduate-level class, people are very responsible. But I could see that being a problem in low-level classes where people don't have that degree of self-motivation and direction to do so.
>
> I mean, my pet peeve is the whole discussion section. Very often that is just kind of people summarizing stuff. That is not truly a discussion. And typing takes so much longer than talking. You never have a chance to clarify something in real time so it's kind of nice to learn how to summarize and articulate in writing, but it's not really to the level of discussion here that you really exchange kind of arguments. A lot of the times the responses (for online discussions) are so delayed that at that time, it's like you moved on because the reading is so extensive that you don't have that much time to engage. People in general are not interested to engage in deep level. They're interested in showing that they read the material, that they understand, that they're thinking about it, but that's not discussing. That's just showing that 'yeah, I read it and I think about it'. A discussion is really sometimes opposing or not understanding. It has a very different flavor.
>
> I still find the interface is little bit time-consuming to get into, but once I'm into the content, it's not bad, in terms of typing it out. The process of going into each object is a multistep process. It's a little bit of a delay to get right in. And the Find function is not good.
>
> I am honest in saying that I think there's a little bit of the classroom experience that you miss, the energy of being able to bounce off ideas, and it makes it more difficult I think for you to connect with other people and share ideas, and I think the spontaneity of the classroom is something that I miss, and if I had my choice, I would prefer to be in the classroom as opposed to being online.

A salient point highlighted in the above quotations is that asynchronous, written communication, though widely implemented, was not necessarily the most efficient way to carry on meaningful interaction for every learner. Reading- and writing-based information articulation, sharing, processing, and synthesizing seemed to be cumbersome and slow for visual and auditory learners. Moreover, the delay between the interaction initiation and response within asynchronous discussion forum catered to the differing learning schedule of nontraditional students, but also discouraged the occurrence of spontaneous, engaged, interactive communication and the associated sense of connection that they valued.

On the other hand, asynchronous online discussions were reported as fostering a digested conversation on the knowledge or information shared. In agreement with prior research on the benefits of online discussion, student participants in this project reported the depth of discussion, ability to learn deeply from a variety of peers, and equity in contributions that was not possible or found in face-to-face courses, as indicated by the following quotations:

> The first thing I would do is read about it (a discussion post). Then I would just let it stew in my head for a while. I don't respond right away. I just stew in my head for a day or two and think about how I'm going to respond. Then I'll kind of formulate the actual working in my mind. I go back and I actually respond to that.

> And I think, again, discussions and feedback actually allow you to explore that much better than you could in the classroom environment. Because you leave, you go check stuff out, you think about it a little bit, you come back, you add your two cents, you know you read what other people are thinking, think about it some more.

Although synchronous communication tools allowed for real-time multimodal interactions among learners, they were not necessarily a better choice for all learners either. Synchronous communication had a more rigid demand on time, resource, and effort for information storage and processing than asynchronous discussion:

> It (chat) takes up more time and I don't feel that I can refer back to what somebody has said, because I don't have it in writing. So for me, it's not as efficient. I can't use the material later, because I have to rely on it from my memory to recall what was said.

> I had construction going on in my house and I wasn't gonna be able to focus on that. So I didn't log in for the chat. But I also had the hesitancy to participate in the chat anyway, partially because I do feel like it's overly head deep and it would have been a difficult conversation for me to have.

It is obvious in the above quotations that synchronous discussion involved a higher pacing and a higher demand on information recall and processing during the conversation, hence posing a challenge for learners with a preference of reflecting on or "stewing" information before response (e.g., learners with an introverted/introspective style or cultural preference), or the ones with less cognitive resources (such as older adult learners).

Sense of Trust and Security in Online Interaction

The student participants who reported a constructive experience of online peer interaction described *a sense of bond or trust* toward their peers – "something that makes it more than discussion, that makes us feel like we're a part of a bigger group… can either cry on each other's shoulders or celebrate." However, as discussed in previous sections, the prevalent practice of online discussion forced learners to interface with peers via mainly written communication. Some learners had reported that they were shocked in a very positive way about how they never got to know peers in face-to-face courses in as deep a way as in online courses, because it was mostly a very few individuals who took up all the "air space" of the conversation in a face-to-face and because communicators had time to think before posting and responding and hence would share deep or meaningful thoughts in online written discussions. The other learners, however, complained that it was difficult for them to get to *know* a peer as a person via only written posts.

More than 70 % of student participants, during survey and interviewing, reported a higher sense of trust for sharing in discussions, and yet a low sense of trust toward collaborative work. They expressed reluctance to become codependent with peers in a team project. They frequently reported frustration when their teammates ignored the shared responsibility and timeline or simply weren't as committed. The sense of obligation, as they described, could be much weaker in cyberspace than in person because:

> You're only thinking of this peer as a name, not a human being that you know; you could easily ignore one's e-mail or chat, but if you ignore one in a face-to-face meeting, that would be considered the height of rudeness.

As a result, they voted to limit the virtual peer interaction only to discussions or peer critiques, which required much less interdependence or coordination of differing learning commitments and schedules.

Related to the sense of trust is learners' perception on the role of peer discussion on knowledge construction. The content analysis of discussion transcripts revealed that online learners generally posted for information sharing and perspective elaboration, with less effort contributed to knowledge synthesis to achieve a higher or new plane of understanding. Frequently, learners confessed during interviewing, "Generally the discussions don't change what I think" and "a lot of times I end up with my same understanding." For these learners, peer discussions helped mainly by "broadening my basis for what I think, giving me more information relevant to a topic" or "giving you an opening." They also expressed a belief that their instructors or readings represented a higher authority or expert than their peers: "Well, I'd probably ask the instructor first, because my peers are all in our same boat," and "when people start throwing out questions during discussion, I get confused again. I'd go back and read the book." These quotations implied that peer discussions triggered or facilitated individual thinking, yet would not necessarily take it in a new direction.

On the other hand, student participants reported *a sense of security* for self-exposure across distance: "People can't see you. They don't know who you are and won't be able to pick you up, so they are a lot more willing to share." For example, in a psychology course student participants were observed actively sharing and confessing deep feelings about a variety of sensitive subjects, such as suicide, drug addiction, and child sexual abuse. When interviewed, they reflected that they became more apt to be honest when they didn't have to sit in front of a person and hence had no fear of being judged. One of them described it well:

> This is why they're (peers) so adamant about that particular topic, or this is where they're coming from because they have experience. I do know them in the sense that at least I can relate to their experience, and that helps me become more of a better listener and maybe more open to different perspectives. Online (interaction) opens you up to more in an odd way.

In other terms, these online learners got to *resonate with* each other via a deep and honest sharing of topic-related experiences, which can be interpreted as the senses of bond and security.

Such a sense of security in cyberspace may be stronger for certain groups of learners, who praised the affordance of online interaction in presenting intelligence via writing rather than physical appearance. One of them, notably, expressed:

> I have a hearing disability and my seeing isn't that great either. I am very, very self-conscious with my disability. The nice thing about online is people don't have to see and I feel that when I come in or face-to-face with people, it makes them think my mental ability is less than it really is. It's easy to interact. I write really well, I have to say. That really helps the intellectual side of it become forth online, but in person because of my speech impediment and my physical disability and being in a chair, I get very self-conscious with people who think I'm less able intellectually than I really am. They won't try to interact with me. I'm not saying they won't; it's just my own thing I have to work on, self-esteem. My self-esteem issues around my disability kind of make me scared to ask for help when I need it. Basically the conversations going online are great. People are extremely supportive and very responsive to whatever I put out. That's wonderful. It makes me want to meet these people in person.

The above reflection quote showed that online interaction had provided a protective, supportive environment to help the student "blossom" without fearing judgment. Similar perceptions were shared by other students who were either "very shy and probably wouldn't say much in a real class" or "extremely disliked arguments or confrontation, and were intimidated by facial expressions and body language in a classroom setting."

The Presence and Role of Culture and Age During Student-Student Interaction

"I think – you know – the more variety you get, the more learning takes place." This comment highlights a common acknowledgement among our student participants of the diversity in online interaction, even though they admitted that diversity made it more difficult to relate. There was a rich presence of culture- and age-related diversity in perspectives shared and the way they were expressed and processed. Online learning enabled gathering of the most diverse learner population, thus allowing an exploration of diversity and opening one up in a deeper way, as the following quotation depicted:

> We have people who were native from other countries. To me, it's just amazing that you probably wouldn't get all those people together in a classroom. And I think a real advantage is the scope of where people are at and their perspective. When you're in discussions, somebody will say, 'Well, when I worked 20 years in New Guinea, this is how things were,' and it's like, wow. Then you ask them questions about when were you in New Guinea? What were you there for? What were you doing there, you know. So I really think it allows you to explore what your culture really is in a deeper way.

A major theme that emerged from the observed and self-reported data is that culture in online interaction is associated with not only one's national or ethnic root or generational custom but also the local community and family in which one lives, their life and work involvements, and hence perspectives and ways of thinking or expression during online peer interaction. A related theme is the occurrence of multicultural exposure and cultural adaptation during online student-student interaction.

Multidimensional Cultural Roots

From survey results, learning activity logs, and content analysis of online discussion transcripts, we did not find significant ethnicity-oriented cultural difference or age-related diversity in the content or quality of online discussion posts. Consistently, during interviewing, few participants voluntarily mentioned their own or peers' ethnicity roots or age groups when discussing their experiences and perceptions of online student-student interaction. Such an observation may be due to the reality that in online interaction, it is difficult for someone to detect another's ethnic or age-related status. Participants instead described and associated their online interaction participation patterns with their life and work involvements.

Cultural Roots in Life and Work Involvements

Frequently, student participants described the influence of career or life experiences on their interaction participation and experience, as the following examples demonstrated:

> Again, one of the nice things about nursing school is that you all come from a similar background. Whereas in other courses, you know, people come from all different disciplines, which, again, is good, because you get to hear and see other perspectives, but they may not necessarily know really how healthcare works, at least here in this country. It struck me again when people say something that you know is at least not true. You know, it's difficult not to say, 'Well, wait a minute. That's not really how it works.'

> I think architects all tend to have similar workaholic, overachiever tendencies. But architects don't have to have good people skills. I've worked on projects as an architect where the whole office stays for 17 hours straight working on something. Now, how many people in my education class would be willing to do that? My other three people (teammates) are going to be willing to do that? They won't do that. They would never have a level of commitment to stay up all night in architecture school like I did two nights in a row working on a project with other people. I'm not saying that that's necessarily a good quality to be a workaholic, but it is something that's part of my personality and it's something that I have applied to my education.

In the above two cases quoted, different discipline-related backgrounds and working styles obviously led to a perceived struggle of participants during student-student interaction. In the second case, the participant shared that her two teammates intentionally ignored her request for virtual meetings and she had to negotiate with the instructor to turn in an independent project instead of a collaborative one.

Some participants associated interaction participation with their growth or living locales or settings:

> I was raised to be incredibly independent and not to have to depend on others. Sometimes it's harder for me to ask people, 'Could you explain this a little bit further?' I tend to spend more time struggling with it. That has affected my learning.

> I think with the culture where we live in North Dakota and the family I grew up in – hard work is very valued. And then you say you're going to do something you do it. You follow through and there's not a lot of sympathy for not putting in your very best effort. And that really influences. The assignment is due on this day and time, and it needs to be in. We're a small community and so I think people always have to be really careful not to let others down in any manner because that kind of floats around everywhere.

> It's really easy to pick out students who come from affluent families as opposed to students who may not. I can figure out if they're coming from the city perspective. When people said, 'Oh yeah, we've got all these choices for kids to become involved so that they're not at risk,' and then there's some that say, 'Wow, I live in an area where there are a lot of poor people, and there are drugs everywhere, and kids don't have those same opportunities,' and that was an interesting dialogue because then of course *cultural nuances* came into the conversation too. That was interesting because it just seemed like it was two ends of the continuum and there was no diversity in between.

These quotations llustrate some of the ways family and local community cultures were integrated into online interaction participation, leading to respect for independence, acknowledgement of diversity, incomprehension toward negligence, or conflictive perspectives on a specific topic.

Cultural Roots in Age-Related Experience and Mind-Set

The online activity log indicated that older learners tended to post more during online discussions. There was also a significant but weak relationship between age and disappointment with online student-student interaction experiences ($r=.08$, $p=.05$, $n=383$). In particular, older learners tended to claim that peer interaction is *better in person.* Correspondingly, older learners tended to report that they interacted with their peers (e.g., named as "book talk partner" or "learning buddy") by phone or even scheduled face-to-face meetings other than web-based interaction.

The impact of age was also observed in the qualitative data. Student participants reported that age-related diversity was obvious in online interaction. They commented:

> I think that's almost one of the things that you can tell more than anything is when you're with an 18-year-old and when you're with a 40-year-old. Just the way they refer to things, the phrases. An older student you can tell by the way that they're very serious and you can't picture somebody a lot, lot younger speaking with that much depth and experience – I don't know you can hear that kind of knowledge.

When asked whether there was age-related disadvantage during online interaction, someone said yes and blamed it on changes in learning settings:

> I think online classes for the older generation are a little bit more difficult because you're used to having that human contact. The younger generation today, that's how they're wired. They're wired for just having the distant relationship with people I think, so it'd be easier for them to learn online.

But others disagreed and argued that it is the age-related experience, convention, or mind-set more than age itself that made the difference. Such an argument was evident in the following explanations and examples:

> I don't think age was the problem, although I do think that there is an age-related mental kind of mind-set… and it's related to mental laziness. So if you, like, say if you're born into a generation where everyone is using an iPod and everyone is plugged into these, you know, text messaging things, you get, so it's a normal thing where it's somebody else would actually have to sit down and learn how to do it from their kid and it's still sort of like 'How could I learn anything from my kid? I'm older than him. I should be teaching him.' I think it was related, maybe not so much to age as to their level of commitment.

> I don't know that I can say chronology has played an effect as much as the time in the program.

> One of our students, she's a year behind me, but she got her master's in the 1970s, and now she's just coming back to school and everything has totally changed. I mean, she used to have a difficult time, you know, about this online environment. I think you do adapt and you get used to it, and she's used to working with computers, but again, I think that learning style, as you said, culturally, and she's Native American, and I think they are more traditional. And so it is difficult to adjust, you know, see something in a text, and work on your own without any sort of verbal feedback.

The above quotations indicated that even though older learners generally tended to be challenged more by the online learning setting, it was mental diligence, learning experience, or intent to adapt that mattered for online learner success.

Emergence of Online Interaction Norms

Over time, a variety of online interaction norms were observed emerging in different classes. One participant commented, "Every class is its own little microcosm of it – its own culture. You know, it's the little language that you're learning, you've got to take it in and feel it out." Part of the class-based cultural norms was related to language and style of writing, which could be in conflict with a learner's natural way of communication:

> Well, it's the type of course. For instance, in pathophysiology, there are some things that we talk about in terms of our experiences, but it's backed up by the research and by the scientific data. Whereas in the theory course that I have, it's much more focused on not necessarily the empirical knowledge, but more on experiences, more on thoughts and ideas. So it definitely depends on the class in terms of the postings.

> And it sometimes can be a tricky situation. Oftentimes I think my comments sort of get away from the theoretical, because everything that we talk about is all theoretic, and I'm much more of a practical person. I mean it's just my own comfort zone.

Part of cultural norms in an online class concerned the convention of correspondence, leadership, or conflict resolution. During interviewing, student participants frequently reported on selecting and responding to posts that resonated with them:

> Well, as far as the discussion posts, I read what other people are saying, and if it really resonates with me, then I post a response. Like maybe I've had a similar experience I can actually speak to or have some knowledge of that. That's the first thing. The other thing is the way the writer, you know, it's the writing style. If it's formal, then I may not respond to that because I would feel I would have to keep my response formal and scholarly. Versus someone who is a little more casual and has humor in there, to me that's a little more encouraging to put my two cents in. This person seems more approachable.

> I picked (whom to respond to) because I thought there was some that I could relate to more than others, and even there were a few times depending upon the subject that I really wanted to put myself in the person's place that had the complete opposite view of what I did, and I found those conversations could be almost maddening in the sense that there was no common ground, and it made it more difficult to continue a dialogue; I felt like I got more out of the people that I could relate to and post on the topics that interested me.

Although student participants generally agreed on the positive role of debate and argumentation when *bouncing or building ideas off* of each other, they voiced their aversion to confrontation during online interactions:

> That (confrontation) shuts me down immediately. You know, like if I just feel like they're really confrontational, I just don't even respond to them. You know when other people are sort of looking at things from a different viewpoint, they continue to just keep driving their point like they're right and all the rest of you are wrong kind of thing. And I just don't respond to those. I just learned that it just doesn't do any good to be argumentative with people who have a certain mind-set. And, fortunately, there's not that many.

Corresponding to this comment was a frequent description from student participants on how they, with time and lessons, learned to express their arguments in a gentle, *appropriate* way.

Cross-Cultural, Multicultural, and Intergenerational Adaptation

Student participants with a guest cultural root (e.g., internationals) disclosed language or communication-norm-related interaction issues:

> For me, it's different because it's taking me so much time to process all that information, more time than the others who are speaking English. It really sucks that I have all this foreign language. When they say, 'Good for you,' they don't mean really good for you. They mean the opposite of that. I know that people may think that 'She's not that good in English,' and that can be a conflict point when you are doing group work.

> We tend not to be politically correct in Brazil. Most of the time we go to the politically incorrect side and make fun of it, and so this is stuff that sometimes I try to make myself really conscious not to do during online discussion.

At the same time, they also demonstrated a high degree of forbearance to cross-cultural situations: "That's fine. I am just playing a game; I am going to achieve it and make as little enemy as possible."

Forbearance and adaptation to cultural difference in communication were also voiced by students with a host cultural root, as indicated by the following quotations:

> One man, and I do continue to read his, and his name suggests that he is not from this country. I'm very anxious to see if that's just cultural differences and maybe he thinks differently. But the instructor loved it (his post), you know, lots of praise and encouragement. That way I think 'oh, my gosh. I'm not getting it.' But I just decided I'm just gonna roll with that, because I can't change my brain. As long as I'm getting the credit I need for mine, that's okay. But I do still continue to just looking on that and say, 'Am I getting – do I understand this stuff more than I did?' No. It could be tied to language, but I just thought it was he had a different understanding of the theory and was able to present them in a way that sounded like – I don't mean to be mean, but it just sounds like a textbook that is really hard, like you have to read four times, like I had to do leg lifts all through reading; otherwise, I'd fall asleep or whatever. I'd lie on the floor and do leg lifts and read his postings, thinking that would help me. I'm curious about those students who seem to be from another country; I'm curious to hear what they have to say and how they're interpreting the material in the classroom. So I'm already annoyed with it and tempted to just drop that, but I do still read it. But I've been to other counties and had very indirect exposure. I would have us meet, if I could. I think what most of this stuff is gonna be only head deep until someone you see in your class or you're experiencing it yourself.

> In another instance, I had a peer student who was overseas and I don't know if it was a cultural difference or not, but I felt it. She was being insulting toward what I had to say. I went online and I just said 'what's going on here and this really hurt my feelings'. It came out in the end that this was more of her way of talking and being. She had not meant anything like that. So there can be some misunderstanding and you have to be very careful and watch for those with online learning. This made me carefully think about what I wrote.

In the aforementioned examples, both students struggled with cross-cultural communications. They both demonstrated an awareness of the cultural difference, an interest in hearing different interpretations, and a degree of forbearance in adapting themselves to dissimilar ways of thinking or writing. During cross-cultural interaction, they felt *annoyed* or *hurt* but also developed a better understanding and knowledge for negotiating cultural diversity.

Notably, in our study we observed the prevalence of students who are bicultural or multicultural. These students demonstrated more versatility in cultural adaptation and tended to view cultural diversity as dynamic, individual rather than static, group difference:

> I'm not a native English speaker. Even though I lived most of my adult life in the United States, I still don't think of myself as an American. I truly think of myself as a bicultural person. Sometimes the difference is somewhat artificial. Other times it feels very natural. It seems to play out more so in terms of how in personal contact actually. I mean, it's often I feel like I'm a little different than others, too. That might also be because they ask different questions. There seems to be an underlying understanding about nursing that everyone shares. But I don't think that necessarily comes out of me being born and raised in a different country. I think that just coming through different personal conclusions.

> Being in the South in this area, I am exposed to different cultural backgrounds and I think that helps me be culturally aware of different people's cultural backgrounds. And just looking at the things that they (international students) post, it just brings a different cultural

> thing, a different level of experience. Again, we all become tunnel vision. We focus on what we see in our lives. But if you read some of the posts that the other students write, then you look at things through a different set of eyes. We all kind of realize that the more that we can learn and communicate with each other, the more we learn and will enhance our learning process, culturally.

> So it (the variety in backgrounds) brings a definite variety of perspectives, different learning modalities, which I like.

Similar occurrences of adaptation were also observed in the interactions among students of different age groups. Having intergenerational peer learners was generally described by student participants as a beneficial setting for knowledge-constructive discussions. Younger students described how insights from older students informed them of the way the world works; offered real, pragmatic perspectives to theory; and hence brought the theory alive. They also reported that older peers contributed a calm presence. Older adult students described their younger peers as bringing fresh perspectives, greater technological experience, and enthusiasm that livens up the learning experience for everyone. They felt that interacting with younger peers helped to dismiss sometimes *jaded* attitudes toward change: "Wow, that's so refreshing because I remember being there, and I remember what that's like, and I need to find that passion again." On the other hand, older adult learners tended to be skeptical about younger peers with immature perspectives and expressions during discussion and their lack of experience that is a prerequisite for forming relational and other connections:

> It is difficult being in classes with only young students in there, because they don't really know what it's like to work and have a family and other things like that.

> This is actually a woman who posted and, I thought, was nonsense. She just doesn't have that much experience in the world. You know, me, with all my age and work. I responded to her and I did it in a really gentle way. I'm glad I was gentle, 'cause I wanted to rake her over the coals for her stupid comment, but I didn't. I wasn't thinking it (her comment) was fresh. I was thinking it was immature…. What I'm feeling is a mentoring feeling, and I want to just help her calm down a little bit. She was kind of up on her high horse over it, you know, which is what someone in their 20s would be. But, you know, I was there. I remember feeling so confident in my beliefs and they were so immature. So I wanted to be gentle to her; I need to tell her that she's really only looking at one perspective, and we need to have a little broader perspective here.

> I think that they (younger learners) were very opinionated and were not ready to see the different perspectives because I think their idea was 'well, this is what I believe in, and this is what I'm gonna hold onto because it's my identity.' I think it's somebody who had more experience being here on the earth have more opportunities to see how different situations play out until you adjust and figure out what's gonna be the best solution or resolution for that particular circumstance.

> I think for those people who have experience, I think it is a little bit unfair. These kids are going nowhere, because number one, they can't write. They cannot connect thoughts.

> I have to always remember that people are younger than me, so I have to gear things toward them to make it more attractive and then respect the fact that everyone has opinions.

Younger students, especially those who lacked rich life or work experiences or lacked skills in written communication, were somewhat viewed by their older peers as mentees or the ones who need patient guidance. A level of awareness and commitment toward cross-age interaction was still apparent in the above quotations.

Student-Instructor Interaction

Age, Ethnicity, and Education on Level of Student-Instructor Interaction

A regression analysis was conducted with the learning experience survey responses to examine the relationship between online learners' age, ethnic status, education level, and perceptions of instructor's support. Analysis indicated that students' ethnic status and their education level (below undergraduate, undergraduate, master, doctoral) significantly predicted perceptions about levels of instructor support, $b=.19$, $t\,(378)=3.80$, $p<.001$; $b=.17$, $t\,(378)=3.11$, $p<.001$. Yet learners' age did not significantly predict their perceived instructor's support ($p=.08$), even though it is positively correlated with the outcome variable, $r=.12$, $p<.01$. Overall, the three predictor variables explained a significant proportion of variance in perceived instructor's support, $R^2=.09$, $F\,(3,\,378)=9.50$, $p<.001$. The result suggested that minority students and students with a higher education level tended to report greater perceived instructor's support.

An ordinal logistic regression analysis was conducted with the survey responses to examine the relationship between online learners' age, ethnic status, education level, and their performance of student-instructor interaction (low, moderate, and high). The analysis indicated that the model explained a significant amount of the original variability, $\chi^2\,(5)=18.70$, $p=.002$. The goodness-of-fit output also indicated that predicted values were not significantly different from observed values, in other words, a good model fit ($p>.05$). The parameter estimate test, specifically, indicated that ethnic status significantly predicted student-instructor interaction level, Wald $\chi^2\,(1)=4.20$, $p=.04$. Minority students were more likely to engage in a higher level of student-instructor interaction than Caucasian students, $b=.42$.

Around 80 % of student participants reported moderate to high levels of student-instructor (SI) interactions. Around 20 % of students reported that their student-instructor interactions were lacking or low in the online courses, due to the following reasons: (1) minimal need of SI interaction (e.g., "If I need help, I know where to find her, but the material is very self-explanatory"), (2) mismatch between students' and instructor's schedule (e.g., "I am not available to chat whenever I feel like I have a problem, due to a family"), (3) need of face-to-face interaction with the instructor (e.g., "*unless meeting face-to-face*"), and, finally, (4) the lack of prompt responses or rich feedback from the instructor. Based on the survey and interviewing results, online students preferred *direct, prompt,* and *private* interactions with their instructors. Correspondingly, e-mail, in comparison to the discussion board or web conferencing, was reported in the survey as the most favored communication tool for the student-instructor interaction.

Technology-Mediated Presence of Instructor

"The instructor is addressing the ebb and flow of the students and guiding, coaching, and instructing" – a citation from an instructor participant

In a face-to-face classroom setting, the presence of an instructor is provided via a composition of instructional *events*, such as lecturing, guidance, practice elicitation, assessment, and feedback (as discussed by Gagné, 1985). Instructional events usually occur within a focused time frame, via mainly face-to-face meetings and oral presentations. The content or activities of these events could be dynamically refined to be individual or group adaptive. In comparison, the distance and asynchronous nature of an online course setting, as the interview, survey, and observation data indicated, poses various challenges toward the design and presence of instructional events. The presence of online instructors is heavily mediated by technologies – facilitation or posting in discussion forums; feedback on assignments in the online grade center; online course announcements; question answering via e-mail, discussion board, phone, or occasionally a scheduled office visit; and virtual lecturing via web conferencing.

Shadowy Existence

The presence of online instructors tended to be limited, especially when online courses were treated by online instructors and learners as correspondence courses in which students only interact with a variety of content objects (Ke, 2010). In certain cases, the presence of an instructor only sojourned with the learning *objects* they prepared, such as personalized lecturing or guidance materials (e.g., notations, video/audio clips). This seemed to turn an online instructor into a *shadow* on the wall ("we know he was there, but we could not find him") rather than an active participant in the educational setting.

Personable Presence

On the other hand, the *personable presence* of an instructor – the exposure of an instructor as a personable figure in online space – was highly appreciated by students, especially those with a high-context culture background (e.g., Latino and Navajo students). The following quotations explained their desire for knowing an instructor's personality:

> I did watch one of the e-lectures that the business instructor did, and that was helpful for me. I just got a better feel of the kind of person he is, and I decided that he wasn't

> drawing hard lines. He's an instructor, he's a professor, he's a PhD, about to retire, and this is his last class. He's not out to make students fail. He wants us all to succeed; he wants us to learn.

> One of the teachers, he used Elluminate, the virtual classroom, and that allowed for much more immediate engagement. And I wish they all would use it on a weekly basis, so that (we) actually have access to the teacher on a regular basis, kind of get into a person-to-person discussion with people. I mean, there's still a delay but at least I have some component of a person. We always get some feedback and, again, it all happens in writing, and I miss that personal component.

The personable presence of an online instructor could be existent via a blend of premade learning objects and/or live occurrences, ranging from an orientation narrative (via a web page or a multimedia piece), an e-lecturing video, a personal notation on the content and discussion, an example of professional experiences, the practice of communal etiquette of first name addressing, and smiley greeting signs in e-mails or discussions to the delivery of web conferencing.

Additionally, individualized attention in course requirements and feedback were frequently mentioned as evidence of being personable, particularly applauded by nontraditional students who were dealing with multiple deadlines and many other obligations outside school:

> They have a little bit of a cookie-cutter approach and she's not like that. The occasions where the instructor forgot to post something or information might be a little conflicting; when this particular instructor thanks students for that feedback and acts on it, that feels very collegial. It goes back to her ability to individualize her comments and the questions that she asks for further reflection. And you feel like you're being given individualized attention, even in very large class where you don't even see each other.

> And so I mean that was a very positive stance of an instructor who wouldn't lower her standards with this but at the same time was very available and did everything she could to help me advance a little bit and, actually, be able to develop a better paper. So that was a real positive stance.

> One of the things that make this course a good course is they all know I (the instructor) individually attend to them. They submit their work individually. I take their Word download, read their homework, and as I read I make comments: "Oh, good point. I never thought about that. Or did you ever see an article on that?" It takes a huge amount of time to respond to those. But that is where my interaction with the student becomes more personable. They feel connected to me based on the level of feedback and the attention I give to their work. The typical goal here is to foster learning obviously. That's my role as a facilitator for learning.

The above quotations, from both students and instructors, indicated that the ability to generate a feeling of individualized attention and a respect for collegiality with students composed a positive stance of a personable instructor. Unfortunately, only 28 % of the online courses in this study, based on the course site analysis and student participants' report, were identified as providing such a personable social presence of the instructor.

Match and Adaptation Between the Teaching and Learning Culture

Match Between Teaching and Learning. When asked whether the current online course design matched their natural ways of learning, around 60 % of student participants reported "yes," 24 % reported "partly," and 16 % reported "no." There was no significant relationship between the response and one's age, ethnic status, or education level. Students who chose to take online courses (vs. those who had to take it) tended to provide more positive responses ($r=.31$, $p<.01$). Students who reported a matched learning state typically reported preference for *self-paced and self-taught* independent learning, while those who reported a partly or fully mismatched learning state generally reported a concern on the lack of live lecturing, personal interaction, and instant feedback from the instructor.

A common theme is that *the teacher matters.* Learners, across ethnic and age groups, described a satisfying online instructor as one who "answered questions promptly (to calm fear or anxiety), gave feedback to the discussions," "pulled out the salient points, presented and engaged (preferably via e-lecturing videos or web conferencing sessions)," and "kept students posted so they don't have to dig for the expectations." On the other hand, online instructor participants, especially experienced ones, reported a sense of being overwhelmed by the demand of time and effort for online student-instructor interaction:

> I do spend a huge amount of time giving them feedback, and I think that's part of why that class is successful. However, I probably need to look for ways to reduce the amount of time I'm investing but still give them the richness of the experience.

There was some discrepancy in expectations on timely feedback and lecturing between online instructors and their students. Student participants recurrently reported a desire for instant feedback within 24 h, whereas a reasonable goal for instructors seemed to be, "to get them back within a week – usually within three to four days." Many instructors emphasized their role as a facilitator who "kind of cross-pollinates ideas during online discussions" and believed that students "are in charge of their learning and are going to get out of the course whatever they want to and whatever they put into it." Less of them prioritized or discussed the design or arrangement for online lecturing. Yet for student participants lecturing appeared to be the most critical part of online instruction, as one of them put, "What I really miss and would love to have is actually a simulation of lecture. And to hear someone present their ideas through, not so much in terms of feedback but rather in presenting and engaging."

Flexibility and Respect for Divergence

> I don't think a teacher can be neutral. I think a teacher is always influenced by what they believe. I learn regardless of my teacher. When I have a teacher who can appreciate a different viewpoint and a different take, then it's just more comfortable. I will not push with certain teachers. While with other teachers I'm comfortable with, I will explore and I learn more.

This citation by a student participant highlights how online students would gauge and explore open-mindedness of their instructors toward diversity during student-instructor interactions. A majority of online instructors in the study demonstrated a degree of cultural open-mindedness toward diverse perspectives and also tended to cater to the needs of nontraditional students, as the following quotations demonstrate:

> She (the instructor) provided readings that are really pushing the envelope, and there is no value judgment toward students' discussions – one can be far out with an idea; as long as he or she can make the point, then that's good.

> These students I (the instructor) know are overcommitted because they've got family – most of them have families. Many of them are single mothers. There're a lot of responsibilities and many of them have full-time job. So I'm extremely flexible as to when they submit stuff. If they give me a legitimate reason, I will extend the deadline for some things even though it says it in the syllabus. I think – just respect for their experience and when somebody makes a really dumb statement, I won't say that's really dumb. I will try to take it and rephrase it and point it out. So I've learned to prescribe time to what we're talking about back to their experience. Everybody's personal opinion is equal. It's the reference that makes the difference.

On the other hand, negative experiences due to divergence were still occasionally reported during student-instructor interactions, as the following case exemplified:

> I'm older, obviously. I'm 52, and I'm dealing with the Internet every day, and there are certain things that I believe are required, and number one, there's a greeting at the beginning of an e-mail. And you either say 'dear' or 'hello' or 'hi,' and I don't know if she (the instructor) means to be, but she doesn't follow any kind of protocol, and she's very rude. And I ask, 'Do I have to do this?' and I'll explain something, and she'll say, 'No, just do da, da, da.' That's it. There's no hello. There's no closure to the e-mail. And I feel like I'm intruding on her time and my questions are stupid, and they're not, and I had an issue.

Student-to-Content Interaction

Time or Frequency in Interacting with Learning Objects

In survey responses, there was a significant correlation between online learners' age and self-reported time on learning activities. Older learners tended to report more hours per week spent online (Pearson's $r=.21$, $p<.001$) and overall course learning activities (Pearson's $r=.35$, $p<.001$). Moreover, learners' education level was also significantly associated with the self-reported time on learning activities. Learners of a higher education level tended to report more time spent on online (Spearman's $r=.13$, $p=.01$) and overall course learning activities (Spearman's $r=.33$, $p<.001$) and higher number of times accessing the course site (Spearman's $r=.14$, $p<.01$). There is no significant relationship between one's ethnic status and his/her self-report time on learning activities.

Correspondingly, the analysis of the online activity log indicated a significant, positive correlation between age and actual time spent on online learning activities. Older learners spent more total time on online learning activities (Pearson's $r=.30$, $p<.001$). There was no significant association between ethnicity and time online.

In the learning experience survey, practice questions, lecturing objects (e.g., presentation slides or videos), reading, and calendar were identified as the most helpful learning objects. They were followed by online discussions. Exams were valued least. The analysis indicated significant correlations between age and e-mails read and sent, and text chats entered. Older learners tended to use course e-mails and text chats more frequently, Pearson's $r=.40$, $p<.001$, Pearson's $r=.30$, $p=.001$. Additionally, there was a significant correlation between ethnicity and content folders viewed, with students of a minority ethnic group viewing or accessing content folders more frequently (Spearman's $r=.18$, $p<.05$).

Content Interaction Processes

Absorption Process

A salient theme that emerged from the survey and interviewing responses was the importance of an iterative content processing or *absorption* process in online learning settings. Online content interaction, with potential reduction in lecturing and lack of focused instructional guidance, tended to be more independent or self-regulated and hence posed challenges to students. The following quotations demonstrated their frustration:

> It isn't face-to-face, but material is still presented to us just like in a normal class, and we are expected to get what is required of us done in a timely fashion just as you would in any class.

> I feel like it (content comprehension) is a mental exercise, an intellectual exercise that I don't get the opportunity to digest with people. If I'm in class with people, I would ask people if it was okay if I sat next to them. It was very interactive, and so from that interaction, I would start to say, 'Oh, isn't that – wasn't that like when we did such and such?' We could digest it right then, you know? And it was information I was taking and applying to my life. Now it's more like I'm taking that information and giving right back in the form of those quizzes or the assignments or whatever that it's only permeating head deep. I don't know how much of that I'm gonna really retain.

> I mean, I like the readings, but I often wish somebody who has more experience could tie them together. I mean, it's just a little bit more upper level summarizing what we do. And when I was in the online statistics classes, (there was) a lot of the frustration, a lot of the crying, the moaning and the bitching, which could have been avoided by using Elluminate. And they could actually use it more.

> I am a visual learner, and it was difficult to understand the material from the amount of reading we had to do.

> What I'm struggling with, with this class, is I want to get out what I put in, I'm willing to put in, but I have all these assignments due every week, and I just don't have time to slow down and think about and respond to people's discussions.

Student participants expressed that their struggle with content processing was mainly due to nonadaptive presentation of content (e.g., only in a single modality), the lack of a partner or agent for information digesting, the lack of external assistance and scaffolding on information synthesis, and the lack of time for absorption due to increased workload of the written assignments.

It was observed that online instructors tended to convert all in-class learning activities in the traditional classroom setting and all course projects into a pack of written assignments and quizzes in the online setting. Although completing these assignments and quizzes could have helped students process the content, they also tended to overload them with multiple deadlines and notably disallow *soak time* for absorption and reflection of the content presented. For example, a student participant explained:

> I just want time to go figure it out. I'm lost – it's not that I have a lack of interest. I'm really kind of in production mode with this now, whereas I kind of got spoiled with all the classes in which I got much more into absorption processing.

Based on our interpretation of the larger interview conversation, this student found himself occupied by assignment *completion* or having to be constantly in rapid *production mode* when interacting with online learning content. As a learner, he was yearning for more absorption time, or more time for the *comprehension* phase during the student-content interaction. Such a desire was also present in other students' comments. In particular, many described content absorption as a double or iterative *exposure* process:

> You have discussions and questions at the end, and then reiterating what you've learned in the PowerPoint, and so you're getting that double exposure to the learning of it. It's sinking in your brain because you keep repeating it.

Interaction with the Content Packet

In comparison with face-to-face learning contexts, online courses seemed to present a wider variety of learning or content objects, ranging from readings, lecturing slides or videos, assignments, to video/audio podcasts, archived web conferencing sessions, and Internet-based resources. All these content objects, as described by online learners, composed a *content packet* and had to be well structured and clearly indexed. A top defining feature of a satisfying online course, as the survey responses indicated, was the clarity and specificity of the content packet – the materials being arranged with a clear outline with expectations outlined for each week – so that "basically, anything that I (the student) needed to ask, I just had to read and I'd find it."

Online students also expressed a desire for the readiness of the whole content packet at the beginning of the semester: "I really want to get that on the first day, get the whole packet," so "I can work ahead or simply plan ahead" and "it doesn't put me in a time crunch with other stuff that I want to do, and it makes it very flexible for me." In general, student participants appreciated the value of the online content packet in *populating the content with a variety of ways to explore the materials* and its accessibility that one can read, listen to, and see it whenever convenient. For example, student participants commented:

> I like that I do not have to listen to lectures, because I have a learning disorder that does not allow me to retain spoken information.

> It (online learning) spreads out the time throughout the whole week instead of 'Oh, class is beginning. I guess I should do my reading.' You actually have more time and you have more spread-out time during the week to think of the subject matter. I think it sinks in better that way.

> She (the instructor) will have a video walkthrough of describing what the essence of the assignment is. The assignment also exists in its written form in a document, where we go through and get the details. I think it helps to have that conversational presentation about it. She's also been very good at making a podcast. So it's kind of nice in that I can download that, and take it with me, and listen to it, you know, away from a computer if the need arises.

These comments suggested that content interaction in online settings, when well designed, is spread out and accessible and awards learners a freedom in choosing their own time, location, and ways to interact with the content. They also suggested that such a variety or multiplicity is facilitative to a variety of ways of learning among students.

When enjoying the preparedness and completeness in the online content packet, students also applauded a degree of fluidity in it, as shown by the following comment:

> It (the content) is open to change as it moves along. I think it's outlined and it's got the objectives, but I think there's a sense of responding and moving, based on the contributions of the people in the class. I feel like it's fluid and not rigid. I think that's probably a critique that more people have of courses that are done poorly – It's pretty rigid.

Such a demand for dynamic content composition got supported by experienced online instructors. In particular, one of them described how he had aligned e-lecturing with the dynamic learning need across semesters:

> It's the problem areas that become the virtual PowerPoints that I put together. And they become more elaborate over the last couple years in an effort to keep things flowing. And I just revise those whenever I see 'oh, this is a problem'. And I try to create that synchronous discussion (i.e., Elluminate web conferencing sessions) around areas where I know there's gonna be problems for students.

It should be noted that the web conferencing tool was frequently mentioned and commended by both online instructors and students as a vital part of online learning interaction. Thanks to web conferencing, an online student was able to get *the immediate back-and-forth touchdown with* the instructor and peers during content processing.

The Older, the More Prepared

Interestingly, older learners, though reported some technical issues, did not view technology-mediated content interaction as intimidating. Instead, their commitment and maturity (e.g., in terms of discipline, autonomy, and self-regulation), gained from years of life and work experiences, contributed to their ability to undertake content processing independently and persistently. Moreover, they tended to report more confidence in synthesizing information because they had more life experience to draw upon.

Archived Content Processing for Language or Culture Learners

Another interesting observation was that the archiving feature of the online content objects put less demand on language or culture learners during content processing. A good example was introduced by a Navajo student, who described:

> In the classroom setting I hear it (lecturing), but it doesn't mean that I always understand it because it's someone from a different culture telling me something. And it could easily just go straight over my head. So, everything that has been taught to me in my culture is all in Navajo and that's what I learned from. And I have to sit there, and process things, and comprehend them in Navajo. So whatever the instructor says will be said to me, and I'll understand it to a certain extent, and then I'll think in Navajo, and then I understand it a little bit better.

It can be interpreted that in the traditional classroom setting, this participant would try to process between languages at the same time that he was trying to listen. And the listening, of course, kept interrupting what he was trying to process. In comparison, in the online learning setting he got to interact with the content materials at his own pacing, with even the ability to look at or listen to something more than once or interrupt to do, read, or reflect, "I read it; I understand it, and then I do it. It's easier."

Perceived Learning Satisfaction

Around 80 % of students in this study "agreed" or "strongly agreed" that "level(s) of learning that took place in the course taken were of the highest quality" and around 72 % of them reported online learning as "successful." Regression analyses with the survey results did not indicate a significant effect of one's age and ethnic status in predicting perceived learning achievement or learning satisfaction of individual online courses. However, the result indicated that ethnic status significantly predicted students' perceived success of online distance education in general. Minority students tended to report less confidence and satisfaction with online distance education (Ke & Kwak, 2013).

References

Anderson, T. (2003). Modes of interaction in distance education: Recent developments and research questions. In M. Moore (Ed.), *Handbook of distance education* (pp. 129–144). Mahwah: Lawrence Erlbaum.

Bernard, R. M., Abrami, P. C., Borokhovski, E., Wade, C. A., Tamim, R. M., Surkes, M. A., et al. (2009). A meta-analysis of three types of interaction treatments in distance education. *Review of Educational Research, 79*(3), 1243–1289.

Gagné, R. M. (1985). *The conditions of learning and theory of instruction* (4th ed.). New York: Holt, Rinehart & Winston.

Garrison, D. R., & Cleveland-Innes, M. (2005). Facilitating cognitive presence in online learning: Interaction is not enough. *The American Journal of Distance Education, 19*(3), 133–148.

Ke, F. (2010). Examining online teaching, cognitive, and social presence for adult students. *Computers in Education, 55*(2), 808–820.

Ke, F. (2013). Online interaction arrangements on quality of online interactions performed by diverse learners across disciplines. *The Internet and Higher Education, 16*, 14–22.

Ke, F., & Kwak, D. (2013). Online learning across ethnicity and age: A study on learning interaction participation, perception, and learning satisfaction. *Computers in Education, 61*, 43–51.

Ke, F., & Xie, K. (2009). Toward deep learning for adult students in online courses. *The Internet and Higher Education, 12*(3–4), 136–145.

Moore, M. G. (1989). Editorial: Three types of interaction. *American Journal of Distance Education, 3*(2), 1–7.

Neumann, R., Parry, S., & Becher, T. (2002). Teaching and learning in their disciplinary contexts. A conceptual analysis. *Studies in Higher Education, 27*(4), 405–418.

Offir, B., Lev, Y., & Bezalel, R. (2008). Surface and deep learning processes in distance education: Synchronous versus asynchronous systems. *Computers in Education, 51*(3), 1172–1183.

Osman, G., & Herring, S. C. (2007). Interaction, facilitation, and deep learning in cross-cultural chat: A case study. *The Internet and Higher Education, 10*(2), 125–141.

Thurmond, V., & Wambach, K. (2004). Understanding interactions in distance education: A review of the literature. *International Journal of Instructional Technology and Distance Learning, 1*(1), 9–26.

Vygotsky, L. S. (1978). *Mind in society: The development of higher psychological processes*. Cambridge: Harvard University Press.

Chapter 5
Cultural Constructs in Teaching and Learning

A working model of cultural constructs in collegiate teaching and learning (see Fig. 5.1) was developed based on a theoretical cross-analysis of anthropological cultural constructs (Ibarra, 2001), elements in multiculturally empowering college classes (Chávez, 2007), learning styles across cultures (Rendón, 2009), ethnic/cultural identity research and theory applied to collegiate student learning (Guido-DiBrito & Chávez, 2003), Indigenous cultural constructs related to education (Cajete, 1994), and an intercultural communications model (Burton, 2009). Within a culturally *integrated* worldview or epistemology, an interconnected, mutual, reflective, contextually dependent conception of the world is common, assumed, and valued. In a culturally *individuated* worldview or epistemology, a compartmentalized, private, outward, contextually independent conception of the world is common, assumed, and valued.

In our 2-year study, we compared student narratives about their learning and experiences in collegiate learning environments with this working model and eight cultural construct continua emerged. This chapter includes an empirically derived visual model (see Fig. 5.2) of eight cultural constructs as well as interpretations and illustrative student narratives of ways each construct manifests in web-based collegiate teaching and learning.

Cajete (1994) discusses Indigenous epistemologies and their manifestation in educational environments. His work deeply expresses the connected, relational, spiritual, and intrapersonal nature of teaching and learning widely found across diverse Indigenous worldviews. Ibarra (2001) offers a theory of cultural *multicontextuality* derived from early anthropological theories of *bicognition* (Ramirez & Castañeda, 1974), *cultural context* (Hall, 1993), and an extensive anthropological study of Latino faculty and graduate students at several major universities in the United States. Chávez (2007) empirically derived a model of six multiculturally empowering college teaching elements including climate of safety, spirit of risk taking, congruence, proactivity, multiplicity, and reciprocity. Rendón (2009) combined a theoretical review of Indigenous teaching and learning practices with a study of US faculty who strive to blend sensing and thinking into their teaching practice

F. Ke and A.F. Chávez, *Web-Based Teaching and Learning across Culture and Age*,
DOI 10.1007/978-1-4614-0863-5_5,

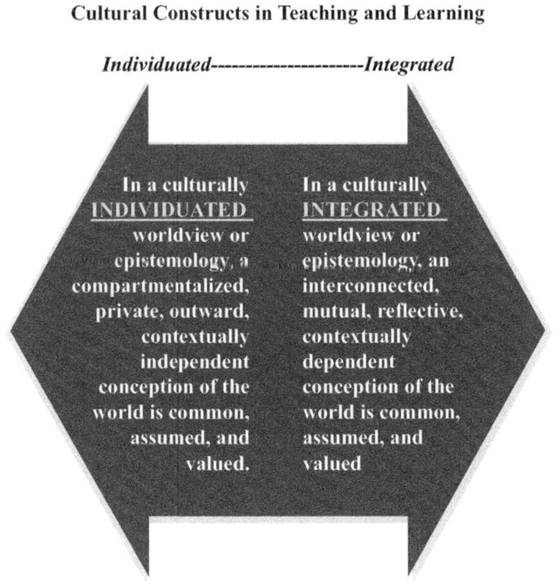

Fig. 5.1 Cultural constructs in teaching and learning

to suggest ways faculty can develop a more culturally balanced teaching practice. Rendón's findings suggest cultural epistemologies are foundational in student learning. The Guido-DiBrito and Chávez (2003) cultural model of learning is derived from an extensive meta-analysis of theory and research on ethnic identity from psychology, human development, and college student development. This model suggests the importance of both conscious and unconscious aspects of culture in student learning; collective and individualistic senses of self; learning through the mind, body, emotions, and spirit; and understanding the need to connect knowledge to students' home communities. Finally, Burton's (2009) cultural communications model, based on a meta-analysis of intercultural communications and anthropological theory as well as research on cross-cultural communications between indigenous health patients in South America and international health-care educators offers an in-depth set of cultural constructs that inform human interaction aspects of this model.

The cultural constructs model we propose in this chapter (see Fig. 5.2) contains eight cultural constructs that emerged from a comparative analysis of student narrative data in our study to the model in Fig. 5.1 of integrated and individuated cultural epistemologies. Each of the eight cultural constructs represents a continuum of culturally based student learning. We believe individual experiences of cultural norms of learning among students may fall in any combination across the continuum of these eight constructs yet cluster commonly for specific cultural populations.

Each continuum in the model ranges between integrated and individuated cultural epistemologies. The *individuated* left side of the model contains cultural epistemologies common and often dominant in US society generally and education

Cultural Constructs of Teaching and Learning		
Individuated In a culturally individuated worldview or epistemology, a compartmentalized, private, contextually independent conception of the world is common, assumed, and valued.	⟷	***Integrated*** In a culturally integrated worldview or epistemology, an interconnected, mutual, contextually dependent conception of the world is common, assumed, and valued
Knowledge, individual competence, to move forward toward goals	***Purpose of Learning***	Wisdom, betterment of the lives of those with whom we are connected
Mind as primary, best, or only funnel of knowledge	***Ways of Taking in & Processing Knowledge***	Mind, Body, Spirit/Intuition, Reflection, Emotions, Relationships
Compartmentalized and separate; belief that understanding how the parts work separately, abstractly, and in isolation will lead to the greatest understanding	***Interconnectedness of What is Being Learned***	Contextualized and connected, belief that understanding how things affect each other within the whole, pragmatically, and within community will lead to understanding
Learning is a private, individual activity, Responsible for one's own learning so that others are not burdened	***Responsibility for Learning***	Learning is a collective, shared activity, Responsible for one's own and others' learning
Linear, task oriented, can be measured and used, to be on time shows respect	***Time***	Circular/seasonal, process oriented, dependent on relationships, to allow for enough time shows respect
Provider and Evaluator of Knowledge -- best perspectives and ways of learning, predetermined/bounded learning; Communication primarily between teacher and students	***Role of the Teacher / Control***	Facilitator of Learning Experiences -- multiple perspectives and ways of learning, emergent/constructivist; wide variety of interactions between students, and between teacher and students
Others' perspectives are optional for learning. Primarily rely on verbal messages; individuals are paramount, few streams of communication	***Student Interactions***	Others' perspectives are important to learning. High use of nonverbals, collective as paramount & multiple streams of communication
Learning by mastering abstract theory first, followed by testing. Rarely includes application /experience/doing in real life	***Sequencing***	Learning by doing, listening to others' experiences or experiencing first, then drawing out abstract theory
Chávez, Ke & Herrera (2009). An earlier version of this model was presented in a paper at the 2009 ASHE Conference		

Fig. 5.2 Cultural constructs model

specifically (Fried, 1994). Individuated constructs tend to originate specifically in a Northern European cultural foundation (Katz, 1985). This is significant for understanding the cultured nature of teaching and learning because current academic epistemologies of US higher education also originate in Northern European cultural paradigms (Ibarra, 2001; Rendón, 2009).

Findings from this study as well as anthropological and educational anthropology theory noted previously suggest that the *integrated* right side of the model contains cultural epistemologies that are more common to both Hispanic and Native American college students (Cajete, 1994; Grande, 2004; Ibarra, 2001; Ke, Chávez, & Herrera, 2009; Mihesuah & Wilson, 2004) and may also be common to especially Indigenous groups in Southeast Asia, Africa, Australia, and New Zealand as well as Latino groups originating in Southern Europe, South and Central America, and Mexico. Some aspects of integrated cultural constructs of learning may be common among African American students with similar cultural origins. Exploration into cultures and students originating in the Middle East is likely to reveal many similarities with an integrated epistemology of learning. The strength of cultural constructs for individual students may be related to how much students are immersed in their own cultural communities while being raised though may have little to do with how conscious they are of their own cultural epistemologies (Guido-DiBrito & Chávez, 2003). Even when unconscious, cultural norms pass from generation to generation through disseminated values, beliefs, assumptions, and behaviors in parenting, community activities, education, and religious/spiritual activities.

Findings: Cultural Constructs of Teaching and Learning

Findings from this study suggest cultural constructs underlie student learning and faculty teaching. Most students in our study struggled to make conscious connections between culture and learning yet their narratives about learning processes, teaching strategies, assignments, rhetoric, and interactions revealed marked cultural distinctions between Native and Hispanic American students who showed learning preferences and norms primarily along the integrated end of the cultural continuum and Northern European Caucasian American students who showed learning preferences and norms primarily along the individuated end of the cultural continuum.

Findings from cultural analysis in this study are summarized and illustrated in the following subsections for each of the eight cultural constructs of the model including purpose of learning, ways of taking in and processing knowledge, interconnectedness of what is being learned, responsibility for learning/space/privacy, time, role of the teacher/control, student interactions, and sequencing (see Fig. 5.2). We believe each of these epistemological and pragmatic orientations is important to teaching and learning across cultures and that much greater application of integrated forms of pedagogy, facilitation, interactions, and climate factors is necessary to promote equitable education and maximize learning and academic success among all cultural populations.

For a balance of cultural emphasis, we purposefully alternated integrated and individuated sides of this continuum as we proceeded through the eight cultural constructs of teaching and learning in the model.

Purpose of Learning

Purpose of learning		
Knowledge, individual competence, to move forward toward goals and not be a burden to society	↔	Wisdom, betterment of the lives of those with whom we are connected

Purposes of learning shared by students ranged from learning for knowledge, individual competence, and professional goals to learning for wisdom and the betterment of the lives of those with whom students are connected and responsible. Though purpose of learning was not specifically asked about in this study, students often discussed ways in which learning plays a role in their lives. Northern European Caucasian American students were more likely to discuss knowledge for its own sake as well as gaining knowledge in the pursuit of educational and professional goals, while Native and Hispanic American students were more likely to connect education to making a difference in their extended families, home communities, and/or tribes. Though most students struggled to make substantive, conscious connections between culture and learning, many described values about the purpose of education taught to them by family that seem to differ across cultures.

Integrated Purpose of Learning Among Hispanic, Native, and Mestizo Students

A developmental journey toward wisdom and a determination to benefit other members of one's "people" (tribe, culture, extended family) with a college education are common among Native, Hispanic, and Mestizo American students in this study. A student self-identifying as Mestizo (a mix of Native- and Latin-based cultures) described wisdom as an important purpose of education yet contrasted this with what she sees as actually happening in her college experiences:

> Wisdom is something we must develop all of our lives, and college offers a chance to broaden my horizons and learn from the wisdom of more than just my own people; though it does seem like the way college is structured, it is not about wisdom but about knowledge and individual attainment which means I must often find the lessons of wisdom myself and with my family.

For another Native American student, "I can't give up. My people, all those who come after me, are counting on me to finish this degree and come home to serve." Similarly for a Hispanic American student:

> I was taught that I have a responsibility to my family and to my people. Even now while I am in college, I must send whatever money I can home to help support my family, and my tios and tias (uncles and aunts) never let me forget that I am here in college to become more prepared to serve my extended family and community.

Individuated Purpose of Learning Among Northern European Caucasian Students

Individual self-reliance, fairness, and determination to work toward individual goals show up as strong educational values among Northern European Caucasian American students, which is consistent with earlier work on "The Components of White Culture" model by Katz (1985). Among students within this cultural epistemological orientation, there is little to no mention of others in their narratives about learning, education, or purposes of education in their lives. There seems to be a belief that in focusing on the self in terms of education and success, an individual is doing what is good and right for society by not becoming a burden on others. One Northern European Caucasian student characterized this sense of purpose of education and individual responsibility for education in the following manner:

> I grew up in a pretty much all White, middle class neighborhood; I mean, I think one thing I learned at an early age was that my education mostly is my responsibility, benefits me alone, and nobody can motivate me other than myself. I have carried that with me through college as well as in the master's program. I shouldn't expect anyone else to do it for me because it's my education. The grades I get are a result of the work I do and will help me to reach my own goals.

Another Northern European Caucasian student explained aspects of this kind of individuated cultural orientation about the purpose of education. The greater good is interpreted within a sense of individual responsibility:

> My career goals are my reason for being in college. I need to be able to take care of myself so that others don't have to. I was taught by my parents that my career and my determination to succeed are good not only for me but for society because then I won't be a burden on others. Even if my career only seems to serve me, I'm doing good because I'm taking care of myself.

A third Northern European Caucasian student discusses her education in relation to individual fairness and hard work within an American dream:

> I think if I work hard I should and I will succeed and education is one of the first places where this happens. I'm going to go out after I graduate and my hard work will once again be the reason for my success. So when I succeed, it will be because of my hard work and I will have gotten to where I am through my own efforts. That seems really fair to me and I'm glad the American educational system allows this for me.

Ways of Taking in and Processing Knowledge

Ways of taking in and processing knowledge		
Mind as primary, best, or only funnel of knowledge	⟷	Mind, body, spirit/ intuition, reflection, emotions, relationships

Students in this study shared a variety of ways of taking in and processing knowledge. In discussing this, there were distinct differences between Hispanic, Native, and Mestizo students and their Northern European Caucasian peers. Learning and processing through the mind were characterized as the best, primary, or even the only way to learn by many Northern European Caucasian students, while most Hispanic, Native, and Mestizo American students described using a variety of ways of taking in and processing knowledge such as the body, spirit, intuition, emotions, mind, relationships, and reflection as essential to any kind of understanding or learning.

Individuated Ways of Taking in and Processing Knowledge Among Northern European Caucasian Students

Northern European Caucasian American students often characterize learning as a "process of the mind," prioritizing thinking, cognitive processing, and intellectual analysis. A Northern European Caucasian student shared:

> My mind is the center of my learning so I try to cultivate my mind in as many ways possible like reading, solving logic problems, studying, and talking with others about ideas. The other parts of me are for taking a break like going to play basketball or laughing at a movie.

Another student went further to specify the need to screen out information coming in from other parts of herself and the urgency with which she was encouraged to do this by parents and teachers if she was to learn and be successful:

> I was taught to quiet the rest of me, my emotions, and my bodily needs to allow the higher order intellectual part of me to take over. Sometimes these teachings were so strong. My parents and teachers made it seem like my body, emotions, and spirit were more than a distraction that they could be dangerous to my mind, my learning, and my eventual success.

Another discussed pressure she experienced from others to prioritize the mind yet questioned this for herself, pointing to this being a learned priority and one that perhaps should be questioned:

> All through my education, my teachers and family have encouraged me not to trust my emotions or my intuition, to ignore these in favor of what my logical mind is telling me. They always talked about emotions and intuition as if it was some sort of dangerous thing that would distract me from the real world. Sometimes I feel like I should question this because my emotions and intuition offer me important information in my life and even in college.

Northern European Caucasian students described a fairly prescribed, narrow range of learning context and process. Most discussed a common sequence of listening to class lectures, reading the book, taking extensive notes and/or highlighting key ideas, and taking exams/doing papers or projects to show knowledge to professors. One student described his process as a common one:

> It has been drilled into me…listen to the lecture, study and read, cram for an exam, write a paper, show what I know, get my grade, and move on to my next class. It is not very interesting most of the time but I know it is what I have to do to get my degree and get ahead. I don't think about it much. I just do it.

Few discussed other means of taking in knowledge, connections of their learning to the world outside of academia, or the use of other senses to learn. This lack of connection was notably absent among Northern European Caucasian students yet a few did question the usefulness of this kind of learning process for their futures:

> I wonder sometimes what good it does for me to just churn out grades and classes to get my degree. Won't I need more to be effective in future jobs and life? I know that most of my classmates just memorize for tests and do little in the way of learning. I do too and I wonder if my college learning experience could have been about more than just getting the degree.

Integrated Ways of Taking in and Processing Knowledge Among Hispanic, Native, and Mestizo Students

In contrast, Native and Hispanic American students often described taking in knowledge through multiple senses and connecting knowledge to the world around as essential to their learning and to determining the worth of specific knowledge. Most described this as something learned from parents, family, tribe, and sometimes from early educational environments within their cultural communities. Some students discussed the contrast between their own natural tendencies for multiple ways of learning with their experiences of learning in formal educational contexts:

> You know it's funny that you ask because just last semester, I took a class where my professor asked us to constantly connect our own personal experiences to the various aspects of the subject during online written discussions. I remember thinking that I spent 18 years of school trying to force myself not to make these connections because this was thought of as personal and so somehow less than, and now I'm finally being rewarded for my own way of thinking and learning in one class. Hmm…I wonder if this is because my professor is Hispanic like me?

Native American students and many Hispanic American students in this study were more likely to discuss knowledge as taken in through a variety of means such as through time in nature and through many senses and connections. A Hispanic American student discussed a wide conception and context of learning:

> We make our surroundings our classroom and for me that means that I spend a lot of time intuiting and observing with all of my senses. Whenever I can I touch and taste, reflect on what my dad would think of this, listen to my spirit about what I'm learning, and try to get a sense of what it would be like in my everyday life and work. Then I connect what I am learning with what I am seeing in my community. If there are connections to my people, my culture, this knowledge is important because then it is likely to be helpful to my people.

A Mestiza American student discussed gaining knowledge through visual means:

> I liked the video clip on star rotation. It offered a visual that deepened my understanding. I was raised in the Pueblo and it seems like everything we learned had some visual component. My grandma would show us or my uncle would draw something in the earth or motion with his hands around something to explain. So I was really relieved when my astronomy course had complex visuals to show everything.

A Native American student discussed his appreciation of being rewarded within the grading system of one class for using many ways of showing understanding in assignments:

> My instructor offers extra credit for enhancing with metaphor, models, tables, charts, poetry, photography, drawings, etc. It has always been about numbers and analytical words in my courses, so going beyond numbers and words into other ways of understanding really enhances my ability to understand.

Taking in knowledge through self-exploration and from other students' self-exploration is important to this Mestiza American student:

> I think the way the class was designed and delivered in such an open fashion made it less intimidating…I believe adults really need as much freedom as possible in a learning environment. I would have to say my favorite assignment was the special project that was open ended. When reviewing others' projects I was surprised at how much I learned from other students and how in-depth and impressive their projects were. I learned and I also realized how much I have to contribute to others' learning.

Native American students describe the "hands-on, doing" (bodily/kinesthetic) nature of online courses as more natural to their learning process and point out that within an online learning context they have "more time for reflection (intrapersonal) before responding" consistent with their own cultural norms.

Interview findings also suggest that certain types of learners, those whose ways of taking in information require external processing or immediate interaction such as interpersonal learners or extroverted personality types, often struggle within online learning contexts. One Northern European Caucasian American student said:

> I really struggle to learn when I can't have immediate response from the teacher and my student peers. It actually triggers my thinking to hear others' thoughts. I want to be able to talk with others about what I'm learning and hear the professor in person.

Alternatively, learners whose learning styles tend toward internal processing, contemplation, and reflection, such as introverted or intrapersonal learners, seem to prefer and do well in online learning contexts especially in activities such as asynchronous written discussions that allow time to process prior to interaction or response:

> I love the contemplative nature of many online courses I've taken. I can pause and reflect on meanings to my own life as I am learning and interacting. I can also think first before I have to respond to others in the class.

Interconnectedness of What Is Being Learned

Interconnectedness of what is being learned		
Compartmentalized and separate, belief that understanding how the parts work separately, abstractly, and in isolation will lead to the greatest understanding	⟷	Contextualized and connected, belief that understanding how things affect each other within the whole, pragmatically, and within community will lead to understanding

Integrated Ways of Connecting What Is Being Learned by Native, Hispanic, and Mestizo American Students

Hispanic and Native American students in this study discussed benefitting most from learning processes that facilitate connection between the subject of study and the world around, history, context, and their own lives. Native American students in this study often spoke of the benefits of learning through connectedness:

> When I returned as a student to New Mexico, I was relieved to once again be connected with the magnificence of the high desert mountains. The vast beauty of earth and sky inspire my learning and I find myself often taking my laptop outside to work so that I can keep my thoughts connected to the earth. The other day I spent hours under the fall leaves by a mountain creek responding to student discussions, reading course materials, and working on my assignment. Because I grew up deeply connected to the natural world, rather than being distracted I got so much done and felt like I offered greater insights to my peers because I felt very centered.

Being able to place learning in historical context and return to previous course materials is seen as similar to oral history and learning from teaching stories repeated often within home communities. One Native American student describes:

> I find it really helpful to go back through the historical archive of the course to review lectures, videos, discussions, even class sessions. It is in my nature to want to reflect on the history of things, to pay attention to the rhythm and context of information in the class. Online courses allow me to do this because usually the professor leaves materials available to students all semester. It is kind of like listening to the stories of our elders over and over again.

A Hispanic student discussed this in similar ways:

> I always love helping my grandma make tortillas because she tells me stories of her life and stories that I can tell are meant to teach me to be a good person and do the right things in my life. Good online classes feel similar somehow. A good professor will introduce new concepts through story or case study or example. Then I can go back and reread these introductions when I'm confused by the more abstract theory. This continual access to materials and stories is not available in my regular courses and I'm on my own to struggle from memory.

Hispanic and Native American students especially those in rural areas often identify online learning as providing a way for them to integrate their learning with the world around them. In their own communities, they are more able to make connections assisting them to understand what they are learning through college courses in deeper, more pragmatic ways. One Mestizo student shared:

> It helps me that I'm working in my hometown, taking online courses, raising my family. I can constantly connect what I'm learning in my classes to my own life, talk with my family about something I don't understand, and even let something sit in my head for awhile while I fix my car. This helps me to get it you know.

Individuated Ways of Connecting What Is Being Learned by Northern European Caucasian American Students

Northern European Caucasian American students in this study described a more compartmentalized way of thinking about teaching and learning. One student explained:

> Yeah, I like thinking about things in removed kinds of ways. I feel safer that way and more like I can work to understand without the pressure of how it matters or who will be affected. Then once I know what I'm doing, it helps to begin considering how it will work in a real situation.

Another Northern European Caucasian American student discussed the importance of understanding the parts before considering the whole:

> I think if we can understand the discrete components of something, we will be better equipped to understand the whole later. I get confused when professors try to describe the whole thing. It is too complex for me and anyway, I'm more interested in how the parts work.

One student talked about what their priority is in learning.

> I think it is a waste of time to think about whole systems. We can never really understand something that way because it is so complex. We need to take things apart and understand how they tick.

Responsibility for Learning

Responsibility for learning		
Learning is a private, individual activity, responsible for one's own learning so that others are not burdened	⟷	Learning is a collective, shared activity, responsible for one's own and others' learning

Conceptions of responsibility for learning differ substantially between Native and Hispanic American and Northern European Caucasian American students. Individual self-reliance and responsibility primarily to self in a learning environment characterize Northern European Caucasian American student responses, while a deep sense of responsibility for peers and peer learning is common among Native, Hispanic, and Mestizo American students in this study.

Individuated Sense of Responsibility for Learning Among Northern European Caucasian American Students

Northern European Caucasian American students discuss the need to focus on your own needs sometimes from a competitive standpoint and sometimes from a sense of taking care of yourself so others do not have to take care of you. Working together with other students is usually seen as a distraction, a bother, or a waste of time. One student describes the common individual nature of online learning as consistent with their individual orientation:

> I was taught that I was all I had and I'd need to rely on myself in school. With online learning, I mean, it has been a helpful thing in that the work is still independent online and so individually focused that, you know, it's kind of in line with what I already do.

Another student describes peer interactions as a waste of time:

> I really just learn from the teacher and the materials. I get frustrated with student comments about what we are learning. It is really a waste of time and I would rather I didn't have to deal with this but some instructors think discussion is a good thing. It hasn't been for me.

Integrated Sense of Responsibility for Learning Among Hispanic, Native, and Mestizo Students

Hispanic and Native American students in this study mostly felt what one characterized as "Multiple perspectives of other students help me to learn the material better." Most shared that requirements to engage in class discussions online are helpful to their learning and to others' learning:

> I have an English composition class on the web where we are required to not only review each other's papers but discuss each and how it could be better. This helps me to be a better writer and I also learn how I might think differently about something and how that is helpful to me and to others.

This Hispanic American student finds that expansion of resources and knowledge through interaction with other students can be helpful to her motivation and learning:

> I really like seeing how my peers get more and more excited about the possibilities of online learning and start to bring in resources. Websites, online articles, and photographs make such a difference in my own learning. The first time I saw this kind of posting from another student, I couldn't wait to go searching for myself.

Hispanic, Mestizo, and Native American students often feel a sense of responsibility for helping their peers to learn and be successful. One Mestizo student described this:

> I've really benefitted from other student's help in my online classes, and I want to make sure I'm there for them too. When I was growing up, I was the oldest boy in my family and it was part of the expectation of my parents that I always be there to make sure my younger siblings were okay and doing what they needed. I see it kind of like that. I need to reach out and offer help when someone is struggling in my classes. It is easy to do this in an online class because we can stay in contact through the site all the time.

Group assignments, however, differ markedly from group discussions and other forms of learning responsibility in online courses. Students, regardless of culture, suggest against online group assignments indicating "conflict of schedules and working styles," "miscommunication," "difficulty having a time to count on for finding others," and "lack of trust concerning team projects without face-to-face meetings" as significant barriers.

Time

Time		
Linear, task oriented, can be measured and used, to be on time shows respect	⟷	Circular/seasonal, process oriented, dependent on relationships, to allow for enough time shows respect

Time and how time is conceived is an important component of teaching and learning across cultures. In a traditional 50–75 min class session, time is highly bounded and most faculty use every minute to share knowledge with students through lectures (Rendón, 2009). In online courses, students have time to reflect between most learning activities; for example, in asynchronous written discussions, there is time enough for everyone to contribute because students can post anytime 24 hours a day before instructor deadlines. This also allows students to work when they do academics best and work within busy schedules.

Integrated Sense of Time Among Hispanic, Native, and Mestizo Students

Native and Hispanic American students in this study discuss the incongruence between highly time-oriented traditional classes and their own sense of time as less structured, based in relationships, and taking the time needed instead of the time assigned. For Native American students, time to allow for internal processing through reflection, dreams, and prayer is considered essential to deeper levels of learning:

> When I can't seem to grasp something in one of my classes, I go sit under a tree or go for a run and let my mind wander for a while. When I return, I often understand. It is as though my mind needed time to process in a different way so that I could learn.

For Hispanic American students, time is often highly relational and also less bounded:

> Time is a funny thing where I am from. We say we are from the "Land of Mañana," the land of tomorrow, because we believe that life moves as it needs to move. This is especially true of relationships and learning. What this often means for me as a college student is that I need the flexibility to move in and out of my studies, my family, my work. I need time to talk with a friend about a theory or to ask my mom what her experiences were in relation to a concept. Online courses allow for this time in a different way than my face-to-face courses and I'm grateful for this time.

Individuated Sense of Time Among Northern European Caucasian American Students

For Northern European Caucasian students, time is often conceptualized as bounded and "divied" out between activities. For some, online courses are too intrusive on their time and too unbounded:

> I can't wait for a class sessions on campus to be over. I have other things I have do. In an online course, class isn't never over. I could go into the course site 24 hours a day so it seems like it is always on my shoulders, like I can't get away from it.

and

> Sometimes I like having constant access because it is convenient and I know I could hear back from my professor or another student any time, often though it makes it difficult for me to know how to use my time.

For others, online courses allow for flexibility helpful to busy, constantly changing schedules in their lives. This may have to do with age and levels of responsibility to work and family:

> I'm a mom with 3 kids. I work a full-time job and I'm going to school right now. My online classes are so flexible each week that I can work on them when I can…a few minutes here and there if necessary. I don't have to worry about finding campus parking or childcare. If the Internet is down or I'm having trouble accessing course items, I just accept it and come back later.

and

> You know, I'm trying to be a good family man like my dad raised me to be and online courses just work for me. I'm able to do all the things I have to do and still work on a college degree. They also help me organize my time because they are often organized into some kind of module based on time or a specific component of learning.

Role of the Teacher/Control

Role of the teacher/control		
Provider and evaluator of knowledge – best perspectives and ways of learning, predetermined/bounded learning; communication primarily between teacher and students	⟷	Facilitator of learning experiences – multiple perspectives and ways of learning, emergent/constructivist; wide variety of interactions between students and between teacher and students

Students across cultural groups applaud instructors who share personal experiences, have a high presence in online discussions, and provide tutorial support promptly through emails and/or web conferencing sessions. "Being there" seems to be the top quality of a good online instructor as students often feel "all alone out here in cyberspace." Although certain instructors believe that making instructional content "fluid" and "not predetermined" is helpful for active learning, almost all student participants shared that "well-structured" and predetermined content with clear guidelines on assignments helped them stay "on the right track."

As observed in this study and reported during interviewing, there are mainly two online course instructional approaches. A *content + support* approach is more instructivist and highly structured with predetermined course content and tutorial support. The learning process comprises reading; comprehending written, video, or online class lectures; and completing assignments. Peer interactions represent no more than about 20 % of the students' study time or are completely absent. A *social constructivism* approach sets online discussions and other interactions at the heart of class activity, and the course content is more fluid and less structured. Social constructivist course design comprises reading, interactive discussions for content comprehension, and then completing assignments collaboratively or with peer help (e.g., peer reviewing or collaborative processing).

Individuated Sense of Control and the Role of the Teacher Among Northern European Caucasian American Students

Most Northern European Caucasian students in this study prefer a content and support approach to course design:

> I want to see everything for the semester right away and work my way along a very structured process of learning in the class. This helps me to feel like I'm making progress and that there is a roadmap for me to be successful in the course. I want the instructor to make things clear and serve as the guide and expert, to be there when I have a question.

Another student shared:

> I like checking things off my to-do list, and most instructors have weekly or content-based learning modules that we complete by a certain date. I especially like it when I can see all the content for the whole course at the beginning. It is a bit overwhelming for a moment but then I chart things out and work my way through.

Northern European Caucasian students in this study expect the instructor to be the one who not only disseminates knowledge but decides what knowledge is important:

> I like courses where faculty tell me what the important material is from the book so I can screen out the unimportant stuff. This way, I can prioritize what I really need to know.

and

> It is really great when the teacher give us notes or a PowerPoint presentation that outlines the important material in class. I really don't like it when we are asked to decide this for ourselves. It seems like a waste of time since the professor is the one who knows.

Integrated Sense of Control and the Role of the Teacher Among Hispanic, Native, and Mestizo Students

Mestizo, Native, and Hispanic students in contrast see the professor as having expertise yet want to be a part of learning within and from the whole group:

> I love learning and figuring things out with other students, and I also want to hear what the professor has to say; after all, they have the most expertise with the subject. I think of them as the one who is leading us in our learning but that we have to do our part.

While Native and Hispanic American students show a preference for a social constructivism approach, they also want to be able to look ahead:

> It is more comfortable to me when the teacher listens to what we are going through in our learning and modifies things based on where we are and how we are doing. I do find it helpful though to be able to look ahead for at least the basics.

Many of these students believe that the role of the instructor is more of a facilitator of the groups' learning than a disseminator of knowledge. This seems to be in part so that students are able to compare and contrast various perspectives and interpretations:

> I really need other student interpretations to learn because then I can compare and contrast. The best instructor is one who makes it possible for us to learn from other students as well as from what we read and from them as the teacher.

Student Interactions

Student interactions		
Others' perspectives are optional for learning. Primarily rely on verbal messages; individuals are paramount; few streams of communication	↔	Others' perspectives are important to learning. High use of nonverbals; collective as paramount and multiple streams of communication

Some students interviewed expressed a marked preference for asynchronous written class discussions, while others preferred synchronous written chats and/or class sessions where participants can hear and interact with each other. Mixed responses toward synchronous or asynchronous communication tools may be most consistent with an individual learner's level of internal or external ways of processing. Internal processors who describe themselves as "needing time to think before discussing" seem to prefer online asynchronous written discussions to both live synchronous discussions and face-to-face classes. External processors who "need to chat to figure out what I think" are likely to prefer live sessions where immediate input, feedback, and interaction enhance their thinking.

Native American students in this study preferred more time for internal processing and to be invited individually into conversations or to give a response:

> I really struggle in face-to-face classes because unlike in the tribal schools I grew up in, there is no silence, no time in class to think or draw our ideas or even to talk with one other student before the professor wants us to raise our hand. I find it difficult too that we are expected to volunteer our ideas when I was taught to wait until I was invited into the conversation before speaking. It feels very competitive and disrespectful. My learning takes a toll in this kind of class environment.

and

> I do so much better with online written discussions because of the time I have to prepare before I share my thoughts. I usually do some readings and then sleep on it before I enter into these discussions and then my thoughts are more developed. I feel that I then have something real to contribute to other students and to the professor. I was taught not to speak unless I have something to contribute that is both substantive and hasn't already been shared…and that includes not repeating what is in the book.

One Hispanic American student discussed her relational ways of learning within online interactions with other students:

> I want to learn with others and discussion is one of the primary ways that is done in an online college class. My thinking is better when I can hear or read others' perspectives and go back and forth with our ideas. I was surprised to find that in online classes, I actually get to know other students more because everyone is required to enter the discussion every week and in a regular class, we only tend to hear from a few students who raise their hands all the time and don't really get to know anyone personally. This helps me because I learn best with people I know.

Storytelling or discussing things in connection with personal experiences is seen by these students as more possible in online courses and very important to learning. For Native American students, learning/teaching is often in the form of storytelling especially by elders. In many Hispanic families, everyone is encouraged to tell stories. Among Northern European Caucasian students, though storytelling isn't necessarily thought of as related to learning, many find that when they can connect something to their own lives, they learn better. All seem to benefit from this aspect of especially online written discussions. One Native American student explained:

> In my family, we learn mostly through stories told by grandparents, aunts, uncles, parents, teachers, and spiritual guides. Online I love it when the instructor starts with an example or story to introduce the discussion and then when other students are encouraged to relate something to our own lives. I had a chemistry online course once where we had to try and share something from our home community that was related to each element in the chart.

A Northern European Caucasian student describes:

> At first I was kind of frustrated in online discussions. I thought they were a waste of my time but over time, I began to see the benefit. Everyone seems to know someone with each of the psychological issues we are discussing and the stories come out even if the instructor doesn't ask us to share them. It is like we all have to first relate to something personally before we really understand.

Findings suggest similarity across cultural groups in this study concerning balance between interacting with fellow students via online discussions and other responsibilities in their lives. Although participants generally value peer discussions, not all deem collaborative inquiry necessary for meaning making. Multiple concurrent responsibilities of working, learning, and taking care of family often force students to perform more assignment-oriented activities and be less motivated toward time-consuming, written discussions unless discussions are significantly included in course grading requirements. One student shared:

> This online class takes three times the amount of time of any face-to-face class I've ever taken. I don't think I should have to spend so much time and I just can't, so I pick and choose and if discussion is optional, I usually don't participate much.

Instructors make a difference in student learning experiences through interaction. Students point out that when discussion is structured in simple, individual, rote ways, discussions stay on the surface and often have a competitive aspect to see "who posts the right answer first." Yet when instructors offer deeper critical thinking questions and expectations to interact and comment on peer postings, and support this through grading techniques that motivate students in these directions, such as specific grading rubrics, conversations deepen and increase in learning value. One Northern European Caucasian student laughingly shared:

> If it wasn't for that damn discussion rubric that my instructor created that made me connect to the readings, share an experience related to my comments, reply to at least two student peers, all for points, I have to admit that I wouldn't have participated so deeply. I realize that I wouldn't have learned very much because not only was I having to do this, so were all the other students. I didn't realize you could have such deep learning experiences through discussion in a class. I was certainly not expecting this online.

Native American and Hispanic American students appreciate freedom in online course discussions from immediate cultural "identifiers" and negative nonverbal signals that are present in face-to-face courses, "As a Hispanic female, I often feel like people disapprove of me or think I'm not very smart in face-to-face courses just because of the way I look." Students explain that this freedom from negative nonverbal signals offers them the ability and/or comfort to express themselves, their knowledge, and insights more deeply in online courses. A Mestiza student explains:

> Because I don't see negative nonverbal signals during online discussions, I feel like I am not being judged as much by my peers, and it makes it easier for me to share my thoughts, go deeper, and offer critique more effectively.

A Native American student offers:

> From my experience, there is an interesting dynamic that occurs in online discussions: students feel "safe" to express themselves on deeper or more personal levels. If I were at home with my own people, I would prefer seeing these nonverbals because I would know that others believe in me but here nonverbals are usually discouraging.

While this freedom allows students to express themselves, many still choose to share cultural self-identifiers as the course progresses such as mentioning "*on the reservation*" or "*back east with my family,*" etc.…this lack of pressure from negative nonverbal indicators is helpful to breaking down initial barriers of judgment and allowing students to portray their cultural identity on their "*own terms*" and provide for a more rich discussion that embraces multiple perspectives.

Communication isn't always without difficulty; one Northern European Caucasian American student shared, "Miscommunication made me feel hurt. It may be cultural difference. This made me carefully think about what I wrote." To encourage effective cross-cultural communication, students suggest that instructors could "post 'how to communicate online' rules" or "add more audio web conferencing sessions" that would allow faculty to intervene.

Sequencing

Sequencing		
Learning by mastering abstract theory first, followed by testing. Rarely includes application/ experience/doing in real life	⟷	Learning by doing, listening to others' experiences or experiencing first, and then drawing out abstract theory

Findings in this study suggest that students prefer and may benefit from different sequencing of activities across cultures. Alternating between starting with the abstract theory sometimes and other times starting with a case study, story, or real-life example assists students with a diversity of sequencing needs to learn.

Integrated Sense of Sequencing Among Hispanic, Native, and Mestizo Students

Native and Hispanic American students share a marked preference for first learning by doing (labs, case studies, application), storytelling, and/or examples (contextual or integrated ways of learning) followed by drawing out abstract theory and concepts from these experiences and illustrations. A Native American student explained:

> I don't tend to be able to really get into studying something until I can see the whole picture first. We used to ask our teachers to draw it first or tell a story or give us an example or show us. Then we could all calm down and read about it or take it apart or discuss the theory, and it would make sense because we would keep comparing it back to the whole.

And a Hispanic student shared:

> My mom always described the context of something and encouraged us to imagine we were there. Then she would start explaining each part of the story. Or she would tell me, here is what it will look like when we are finished and then tell us each step. I find myself wanting my professors to do this now, to tell me or show me what things fit into so I can begin to see the significance of the parts or of some theory. I think to myself, what does this have to do with my life?

Individuated Sense of Sequencing Among Northern European Caucasian American Students

In contrast, Northern European Caucasian students seem to prefer to learn abstract theory or concepts (individuated, compartmentalized, abstract ways of learning) followed by application of these ideas to laboratory experiments, case studies, or fieldwork:

> I get really uncomfortable when I'm asked to apply something from class to myself. You know I was taught that it is almost dangerous to go there, to self-explore. So I want to learn the theory and then apply it to the lab or to a case study. I think it is more effective to not get personally involved with what I am learning. I can stay removed and more objective that way. But either way, I prefer to start with the theory.

A likely use of less contextual pedagogical techniques by a largely Northern European Caucasian American pool of professors may be less culturally congruent for contextually oriented Native and Hispanic American students who benefit from starting with contextual stories, examples, case studies, lab work, and simulations followed by processing of related theory.

Discussion

Findings from this study suggest that Native, Hispanic, Mestizo American, and perhaps other students of color in college are likely to reside firmly within an integrated cultural paradigm and practice in regard to learning. Further, it is likely with the Germanic and English Northern European Caucasian origins of higher education and high prevalence of faculty from cultures based within an individuated epistemology that many domestic and international students of color are experiencing a disconnect between their cultural ways of learning and learning experiences in college courses. Based on the findings of this study:

Native American college students are more likely to learn if the learning process includes the following: (1) use of visual models and drawings by the professor; (2) time to make sense of things through visual means – mapping, drawing connections between concepts, charting, etc.; (3) application of course content to self, family, and tribe; (4) time for reflection before discussion and silence during online class time to gather thoughts and reflect on ideas presented; (5) learning by doing, through case studies, metaphor, application, labs, and field assignments; and (6) ongoing access to past learning materials, that is, lecture notes, visuals, and videos.

Hispanic American college students are more likely to learn when the learning process includes the following: (1) learning by doing (application first, theory second); (2) processing with student peers especially to compare and contrast ideas and work collaboratively toward solutions; (3) learning from student peer work including presentations, papers, and projects; (4) storytelling, examples, and illustrations; (5) feeling cared about by the professor; and (6) when professors assist students to connect course content to their lives.

Recommendations for Teaching

To enhance learning and success across many cultures of students, we would encourage faculty to (1) balance instructional activities, assignments, and interaction from both sides of the cultural continuum; (2) assess their own cultural constructs of teaching and learning and their own overall cultural epistemologies; (3) systematically observe how their own cultural epistemologies play out in current pedagogy, relational dynamics with students, and classroom climate; (4) alternate sequencing of learning activities between integrated and individuated epistemologies; (5) alternate starting with reflection and discussion to promote student interaction and balance needs of internal and external processors; (6) develop ways for students to learn from and with other students; and (7) partner with students to figure out new ways of teaching and learning (see Part III for in-depth discussion of recommendations for teaching and course design).

Implications for Future Research

There is rich opportunity for research in the area of web-based teaching and learning across cultures, including (1) a deeper look at learning styles and intelligences common to students from specific cultures; (2) ways to interact across cultures in relation to course subjects; (3) exploration and deconstruction of how instructors cultural identity relates to course design, pedagogy, facilitation, and evaluation; (4) research on instructors who are working to balance cultural constructs in their teaching; (5) study of what kind of facilitation promotes deeper relationships and sharing among students; (6) how varying ways of reflecting and discussing impact overall student success and learning; and (7) how learning from student peer work impacts student overall learning, satisfaction, and success across cultures.

Acknowledgements The Authors would like to thank Felisha Herrera for her work and insights on early versions of the Cultural Constructs Model.

References

Burton, L. (2009). An intercultural communication model. Unpublished thesis, University of New Mexico, Albuquerque, NM.

Cajete, G. (1994). *Look to the mountain: An ecology of Native American education*. Ashville, NC: Kivaki Press.

Chávez, A. F. (2007). Islands of empowerment: Facilitating multicultural learning communities in college. *International Journal of Teaching and Learning in Higher Education, 19*(3), 274–288.

Fried, J. (1994). *Shifting paradigms in student affairs: Culture, context, teaching and learning*. Lanham: American College Personnel Association.

Guido-DiBrito, F., & Chávez, A. F. (2003). Understanding the ethnic self: Learning and teaching in a multicultural world. *Journal of Student Affairs, 7*, 11–21.

Grande, S. (2004). *Red pedagogy: Native American social and political thought.* Lanham, MD: Rowman & Littlefield.

Hall, E. T. (1993). *The dance of life.* New York: Doubleday.

Ibarra, R. (2001). *Beyond affirmative action: Reframing the context of higher education.* Madison: University of Wisconsin.

Katz, J. H. (1985). The sociopolitical nature of counseling. *The Counseling Psychologist, 13*(4), 618.

Ke, F., Chávez, A. F., & Herrera, F. (2009). *Web based teaching and learning across culture and age.* Paper presented at the annual meeting of the American Educational Research Association, San Diego.

Mihesuah, D. A., & Wilson, A. C. (2004). *Indigenizing the academy: Transforming scholarship and empowering communities.* Lincoln: University of Nebraska Press.

Ramirez, M., & Castañeda, A. (1974). *Cultural democracy: Bicognitive development and education.* New York: Academic Press.

Rendón, L. I. (2009). *Sentipensante (sensing/thinking) pedagogy: Educating for wholeness, social justice and liberation.* Sterling: Stylus.

Chapter 6
Online Interaction and Instructional Context Design and Learner Success

Effective instructional design for online learning environments is extensively described, proposed, and examined in the literature. Although still in early stages, the research on designing adaptive and inclusive online activity and learning contexts shows obvious growth and progress during the past two decades (e.g., Branch, 1997; Collis, 1999; Edmundson, 2007; Henderson, 1996; Macfadyen, Roche, Doff, Reeder, & Chase, 2004; McLoughlin & Oliver, 2000; Protheroe & Turner, 2003; Rogers, Graham, & Mayes, 2007). However, instructional or learning conditions for promoting online learning success are still generic and ambiguous and lack rigorous empirical examination and evidence-based support. A potential reason, as Protheroe and Turner (2003) argued, is that "there is no single best teaching method that will effectively reach all students at all times" (p. 3). Approaches to online teaching and learning and hence instructional design usually reflect differing epistemic orientations, values, and preferences of a diversity of cultural, class, and gendered populations (Dabbagh, 2005; Henderson, 1996). Thus it is difficult to propose a standard model of instructional design that can accommodate dynamic needs of diverse student populations.

A critical proposition of research literature on culture- or diversity-sensitive instructional design is to empirically examine the relationship between online learning environment design features and online learning participation and success. In this chapter we focus on describing the salient features of diverse online interaction arrangements and instructional contexts across academic disciplines, and illustrating potential associations between online instructional design features and learners' participation and satisfaction. More detailed discussion and the design implications of the project findings on the online instructional context and the relationship between learning environment, motivated learning strategy factors, and learning satisfaction will be presented in Chaps. 7 and 8.

F. Ke and A.F. Chávez, *Web-Based Teaching and Learning across Culture and Age*,
DOI 10.1007/978-1-4614-0863-5_6, © Springer Science+Business Media New York 2013

Online Interaction Arrangements on Learning Participation and Satisfaction

A conceptual framework for the arrangement of online interaction modes in online courses of multiple disciplines emerged from analysis of course sites, documents, and interviewing instructor and student participants in this study. This framework, outlined in Table 6.1, was used to further examine the effect of interaction arrangements on online learning participation and satisfaction.

Effect of Interaction Arrangements on Online Learning Participation and Satisfaction

Interaction modes of the courses examined were coded based on the framework for the arrangement of online interactions (Table 6.1). Six types of online interaction arrangements emerged from the data: SC+SI+SS (i.e., a balanced arrangement with a moderate level for three interaction modes), SC+SS (i.e., a moderate arrangement level in the student-content and student-student interactions, with no arrangement for the student-instructor interaction), SC+SS+lowSI (i.e., a moderate arrangement level in the student-content and student-student interactions, low in the student-instructor interaction), SC+SI, SC+SI+lowSS, and SC+lowSI.

Analyses of variance were conducted with the learner activity log data to examine the potential effect of interaction arrangements on learners' online participation, including time spent online, number of online course access, type and amount of content objects they interacted with, and online files they reviewed. There was no significant difference among the interaction arrangement modes in reinforcing online learning participation. However, there was a trend that students in a course with a balanced arrangement of interaction modes (SC+SI+SS) tended to access and check the online course site more than those in other courses, $p=.06$.

An analysis of variance was also conducted with the learning experience survey responses to investigate the potential effect of interaction arrangements on learners' satisfaction with online courses. The analysis indicated a significant result, $F\ (5, 372)=2.42$, $p<.05$. In particular, the post hoc pair-wise comparisons indicated that learners in an online course with the interaction arrangement of SC+SI reported lowest learning satisfaction, whereas those in an online course with the interaction arrangement of SC+SI+lowSS reported the highest learning satisfaction. The former's learning satisfaction was significantly lower than the latter's learning satisfaction, $p<.05$. This interesting result implied that the student-student interaction is a necessary component of online interaction, but a high peer interaction level would not reinforce the highest learning satisfaction. Rather, student-content and student-instructor interactions were still the two foundational components of a satisfying learning experience, being enhanced by a low level of student-student interaction. This finding and its implication are consistent with our qualitative findings on students' perceptions of the three types of learning interactions (presented in Chap. 4).

Table 6.1 The arrangement of online interaction modes

Components	Dimensions	Items and/or features	Arrangement level
Student-to-instructor interactions (SI)	Academic presence of the instructor	1. Assignment feedback	Low: item 1–2 presented;
		2. Course management via class emails or online announcements.	Medium: item 1–3+ presented;
		3. Question answering via email, phone, or a "virtual-office" discussion forum	High: item 1–5+ presented
		4. Discussion facilitation: Evaluator, coordinator, wrapper, and/or leader	
		5. Live lecturing (via regular web conferencing or chat-room sessions)	
	Social presence of the instructor	6. Self-introduction page or welcome video	
		7. Video- or audio-based feedback or narrative	
		8. Face-to-face meeting	
Student-to-student interactions (SS)	Social oriented (S)	1. Self-introduction page or post	Low: the initial item of S, RC, or A is presented/graded;
		2. Virtual *café* – a discussion forum solely for social purpose	Medium: 2+ items of category S, R *or* A are presented/graded
	Reading comprehension oriented (RC)	1. Close-ended question answering	High: 3+ items across 3 categories are presented/graded
		2. Semi-structured discussion based on a topic, a case, or a debate	
		3. Open-ended discussion without specifying topics	
	Assignment oriented (A)	1. Peer help or critique	
		2. Collaborative project	
Student-to-content interactions (SC)	Learning materials and activities	Diverse content objects: readings, lecture slides, narratives, video or audio clips, cases, games or drills, etc.	Low: single type of content object and learning task
		Diverse learning tasks: exams, exercises, and/or projects	Medium: multiple types of content object and learning task, presented in multi-modality
		Presentation features: 1. Multi-modality (i.e., textual, visual, and auditory) 2. Simplicity: number of *clicks* to find the right material 3. Fluidity (i.e., preplanned vs. lively updating) 4. Flexibility in deadline of learning tasks	High: diverse content objects and learning tasks, with a good presence of fluidity, simplicity, or flexibility

Note: This table is a customization of the framework on the disposition of online interaction contexts (Ke, 2013)

Effect of Interaction Arrangements on Online Discussion Performance

Analyses of online discussion transcripts indicated that diverse arrangements of the three modes of online learning interaction significantly influenced the interactivity of students' online discussions. Online interaction contexts that prioritized student-to-student interactions (e.g., the types of SC+SS+lowSI & SC+SS) were found to promote more interactive, reciprocal online discussions (e.g., number of responses and number of the online posts responded) than the other online interaction arrangements (Ke, 2013). Correspondingly, online courses of an applied discipline, with a higher possibility to choose an interaction context that prioritizes peer interactions (Neumann, Parry, & Becher, 2002), were associated with more interactive, reciprocal online discussions.

The analyses also indicated a significant effect of the online interaction arrangement on the content or the nature of students' online discussion posts. Still, online interaction contexts that prioritized student-to-student interactions, in comparison to those that focused on student-instructor interactions (e.g., the types of SC+SI, SC+SI+lowSS), promoted more knowledge-construction-related online discussions (Ke, 2013). This finding may provide additional evidence for the report of a prior study by Bernard et al. (2009) that the effect of student-student interactions (SS) was significantly larger than that of student-instructor interactions (SI) (p. 1259). However, it should be noted that online discussion transcript analysis is only an online measure of learning interaction participation and performance. Our qualitative findings (as described in Chap. 4) indicated that online students interviewed did report a critical role of the instructor and instructor-led lecturing or feedback in an online learning setting. The quality of other interaction performance measures (e.g., the process of knowledge construction in synchronous web conferencing sessions and the content of the e-mail conversations) should be further examined to investigate the design and potentially differential effect of online interaction contexts in future studies.

On the other hand, online discussion analysis indicated that an interaction context with a balanced and inclusive arrangement of the three modes of learning interaction (i.e., the type of SC+SI+SS) promoted more online discussions containing the content of self-reflection (Ke, 2013). This positive effect of the balanced approach to arranging online interactions provided supportive evidence for Swan's argument (2001) that the three modes of interaction should function dependently in practice to support the success of online learning. The finding should inspire more future examinations how a balanced integration of interpersonal interactions with peer students and the instructor would facilitate critical or *intrapersonal* discourses (the ones reinforcing metacognitive awareness) (Annand, 2011).

Overall, the finding on the differential effect of diverse arrangements of the three learning interactions did not provide evidence to support a hypothesis of Anderson's theorem (2003) that an online instructional designer can substitute one type of interaction for one of the others with little loss in educational effectiveness. In this project, all online courses examined provided the purposefully designed content package or objects; thus it was difficult to find an in situ implementation of the online interaction context that excluded student-content interaction. Moreover, student-student interaction or student-instructor interaction, as the current findings implied, may have a differential effect on different learning outcomes or be serving different learning processes in the online setting. As such, it is still helpful to consider and arrange for the inclusion of all three learning interaction modes during online instructional design, with the presence level of each interaction mode adjusted delicately based on the needs of diverse academic disciplines, learners, and learning objectives.

Other Salient Features of Online Instructional Contexts

Apart from the online interaction context, other salient instructional design components and features that depict the profile of online instructional contexts have emerged from an artifact analysis with online course sites and interviewing results. These instructional design components, along with their dimensions and approaches, are synthesized in the following table (Table 6.2). The design implications of this online instructional context framework will be discussed in Chap. 8.

The instructor interview and artifact analysis with course sites indicated that the selection of design approaches to delivering each online instructional component was usually influenced by an instructor's individual online education experience, teaching epistemology (e.g., culturally individuated and integrated orientations as described in Chap. 5), and discipline-related teaching culture. In general, it was observed that the more online design or teaching experience an online instructor had, the more active role they played during online discussion facilitation, the clearer or better structured the course content and activity were, and the higher level of frequency and variety (e.g., modality and synchronicity) was observed in the instructor's lecturing and learner support practices. Online instructors of minority status or who demonstrated a stronger cultural awareness during interviewing tended to have more visuals or pictorial messages (e.g., icons or image banners) included in their course-site interface. It was also obvious that online instructors from a *pure* or a *hard* academic discipline tended to focus on instructor-led learning interactions, whereas those of an *applied* or a *soft* discipline, in comparison, tended to act more as a participant or a facilitator during online discussions.

Match Between Instructional Context and Learning Preference

Learning experience survey results demonstrated a significant association between whether the instructional context matched a learner's learning preference and one's perceived learning success (Yes or No) or degree of learning satisfaction, χ^2 (2, $N=354$)$=58.24$, $p<.001$; $r=.29$, $p<.001$. Specifically, online students reporting a

Table 6.2 Profile of the online instructional context

Components	Dimensions	Approaches
Course design	Design of online learning interaction	• Arrangement of interaction modes: presence and composition of student-student, student-instructor, and student-content interactions (i.e., Table 6.1)
	Design of online learning evaluation	• Individual and/or team effort • Off-line projects and/or online, speeded tests
	Design of online learning interface	• Structure of content and activity items: ○ Home page – presentation of the content chunking and sequencing in module, week, or topic ▪ Sublevel – presentation of within-module or within-week learning events ○ Navigation menu – link to major learning aids or tools (e.g., syllabus, calendar, e-lectures, references, practices or assignments, and interaction tools) • Visual design: default folder/text view versus content-themed visual icon/banner
Facilitation and instruction	Learner management	• Weekly online announcement • Individual e-mail
	Virtual lecturing	• Noninteractive lecturing materials (e.g., PowerPoint slides, instructional videos, instructor's notes) • Weekly or biweekly virtual meeting • Podcasting
	Facilitation of online discussion participation	• Instructor's role: leader, facilitator, participant, versus lurker • Timing of discussion facilitation: opening, wrapping, or woven into a discussion session • Approaches of facilitation: evaluation, probing, explanation, or synthesis
	Learning support	• Assignment feedback • Assistance via an asynchronous question-answering forum or scheduled chat/conferencing sessions • Individual help via phone, e-mail, and occasionally in-person meeting

Note: The profile is a customization of the disposition of online teaching presence (Ke, 2010)

matched learning/instruction style tended to report learning success and higher learning satisfaction, whereas those who reported a mismatched learning/instruction style tended to respond nonsuccess and lower learning satisfaction.

Perceived Learning Environment Climate on Learning Satisfaction

A structural equation modeling approach was adopted to examine the relationship between the perceived learning environment climate and online students' learning satisfaction, in an effort to investigate the research model for designing a

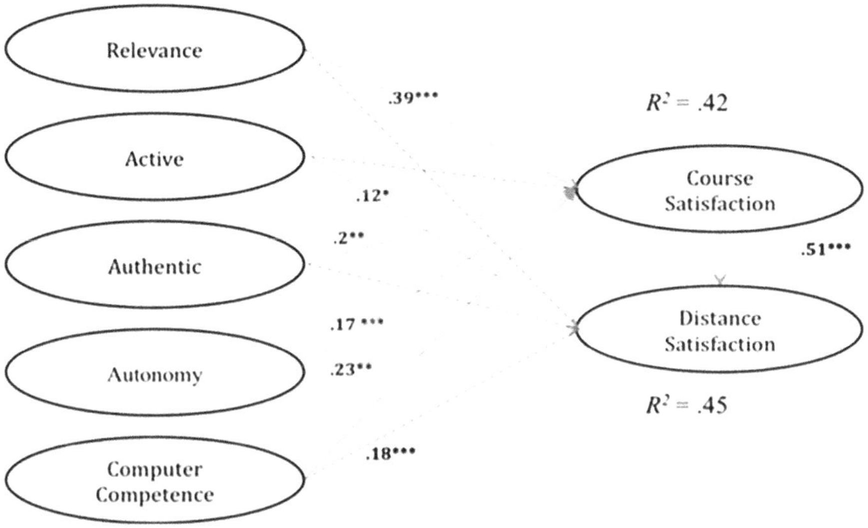

Fig. 6.1 Hypothesis testing results (Ke & Kwak, 2013b) (Note: Path significance – ***<0.01, **<0.05, *<0.1)

multifaceted, active learning environment to enhance online learner success. Based on the design theory of technology-based student-centered learning (Hannafin & Land, 1997; Lea, Stephenson, & Troy, 2003) and constructivist learning environments (Dillenbourg, Schneider, & Synteta, 2002; Jonassen, 1999; Jonassen & Land, 2000), we proposed an initial theoretical model focusing on the predicative relationship between the elements of learning environment climate and students' learning satisfaction. Structural equation modeling (SEM) analysis was then conducted to investigate to what degree the model fits data collected from the learning experience survey. The learning experience survey included a section of Distance Education Learning Environments Survey (DELES, Walker & Fraser, 2005), which evaluated learners' satisfaction with a specific online course, distance education in general, and diverse learning environment climate constructs such as *personal relevance, authentic learning, active learning,* and *student autonomy* (all $\alpha > .90$).

Goodness of fit of the final structural equation model was examined using a list of fit indices suggested by the literature. All model fit indices revealed an adequate structural equation model based on the standard suggested by Bogozzi and Yi (1988) and Marsh, Hau, and Wen (2004): χ^2/d.f. = 2.14; RMSEA = .05; AGFI and GFI > .8; IFI, TLI, and CFI > .9 (Ke & Kwak, 2013b). It was concluded that the structural equation model had a good fit with the study data.

Results of the analysis for the structural model are presented in Fig. 6.1 (Ke & Kwak, 2013b). The estimated path coefficient (standardized) and its associated significance level are specified next to each link. The R^2 statistic is indicated next to the endogenous construct. Results indicated that the model explained 42 % of the variance in course satisfaction and 45 % of the variance in distance education satisfaction.

The learning environment climate of *personal relevance* positively influenced students' online course satisfaction ($\beta = .39$, $p < 0.01$) and had an indirect effect on their satisfaction with online education in general ($\beta = .2$). The learning environment climate of *active learning* positively influenced students' online education satisfaction ($\beta = .12$, $p < 0.1$). The learning environment climate of *authentic learning* positively influenced students' online course satisfaction ($\beta = .2$, $p < 0.05$) and had an indirect effect on their satisfaction with online education in general ($\beta = .1$). The learning environment climate of *student autonomy* positively influenced students' online course satisfaction ($\beta = .17$, $p < 0.01$) and their satisfaction with online education in general ($\beta = .23$, $p < 0.05$). Students' computer competence also positively mediated students' online course satisfaction ($\beta = .18$, $p < 0.01$) and had an indirect effect on their satisfaction with online education in general ($\beta = .09$). Online course satisfaction positively influenced the satisfaction toward online education in general ($\beta = .51$, $p < 0.01$).

Association Among Motivated Learning Strategies, Learning-Instruction Matching, and Learning Satisfaction

The learning experience survey results indicated that motivated learning strategies of online students predicted their perception of learning-instruction-style matching and hence their online course satisfaction. Among the motivational orientations and diverse cognitive and metacognitive learning strategies measured via the MSLQ, intrinsic motivation and the use of metacognitive self-regulation were found to have a significant predictive effect on online learners' perception of the match between their learning preferences and the instructional context and hence their satisfaction with the online course. The factors' regression weights are outlined in Tables 6.3 and 6.4.

A structural equation modeling approach was then adopted to further investigate the structural model on the relationship among the aforementioned constructs (see Fig. 6.2). Table 6.5 indicated goodness-of-fit information for this structural model.

Figure 6.3 and Table 6.6 indicated the significant direct and indirect effects of the variables of intrinsic motivation, self-regulation, and computer competence on students' perception on the match between their learning preferences and the online instructional context and their online course satisfaction in the proposed research model. Results indicated that the model explained 79 % of the variance in online course satisfaction. The two motivated learning strategy factors (intrinsic motivation and self-regulation) had a significant direct impact on both learning-instruction match ($\beta = .31$, $p < 0.05$; $\beta = .39$, $p < 0.01$, respectively) and online course satisfaction ($\beta = .24$, $p < 0.01$). The variable of the learning-instruction match had a significant positive direct effect on online course satisfaction ($\beta = .58$, $p < 0.01$). The result suggested that intrinsic motivation and self-regulation both directly and indirectly influenced learning satisfaction. The match between learning preference and instructional context served as a mediator for the indirect relationship between strategy factors and online course satisfaction. Learners' computer competence, in comparison, only had a direct effect on course satisfaction ($\beta = .44$, $p < 0.05$).

Table 6.3 Regression weights

			Estimate	S.E.	C.R.	*P*
Match	←	Intrinsic motivation	.47	.08	1.97	0.036
Match	←	Self-regulation	.56	.06	2.11	0.003
Match	←	Computer competence	.74	.28	.22	.86
Online course satisfaction	←	Intrinsic motivation	.36	.08	15.75	<.001
Online course satisfaction	←	Self-regulation	.38	.09	10.86	<.001
Online course satisfaction	←	Computer competence	.53	.07	1.96	.02
Online course satisfaction	←	Match[a]	.87	.12	5.94	<.001

Note: [a]Online learners' perception on the match between their learning preferences and the instructional context

Table 6.4 Standardized regression weights

			Estimate	*P*
Match	←	Intrinsic motivation	.31	.04
Match	←	Self-regulation	.39	.003
Match	←	Computer competence	−.01	.86
Online course satisfaction	←	Intrinsic motivation	.24	<.001
Online course satisfaction	←	Self-regulation	.24	<.001
Online course satisfaction	←	Computer competence	.44	.02
Online course satisfaction	←	Match	.79	<.001

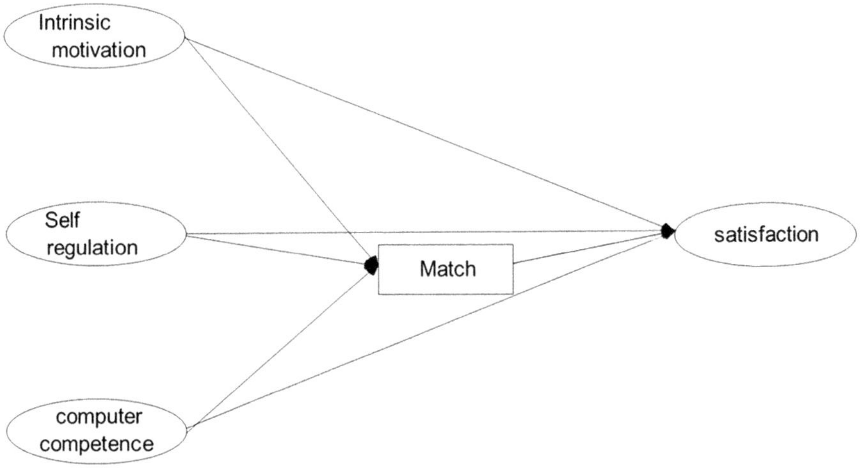

Fig. 6.2 The structural model

Table 6.5 Goodness of fit

Fit indices	Criteria	Result/value
χ^2 statistic	Insignificant	Insignificant
χ^2/d.f.	<3	1.76
RMSEA	<0.08(with CFI of 0.9 or higher)	.08
GFI	>0.9	.91
AGFI	>0.8	.85
IFI	>0.9	.94
TLI	>0.9	.90
CFI	>0.9	.94

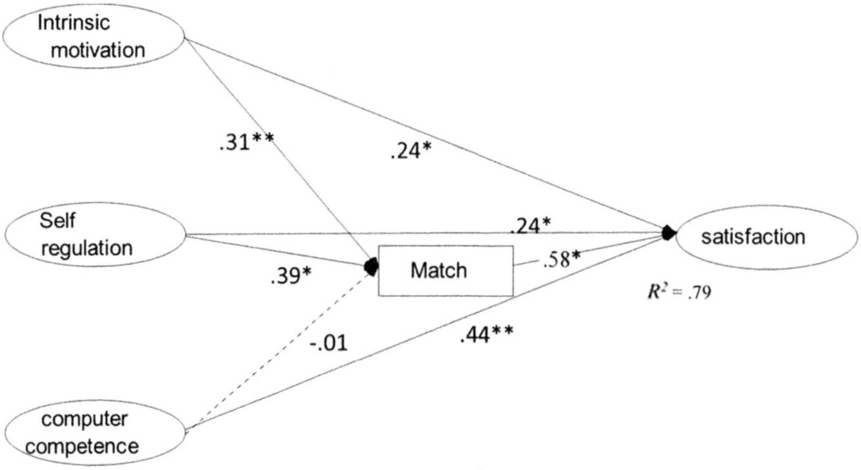

Fig. 6.3 Hypothesis testing results Note: Path significance – $*p<0.01$; $**p<0.05$

Table 6.6 Effect of motivated orientation and self-regulation on online learning satisfaction

	Match		Satisfaction	
	Direct effects	Indirect effects	Direct effects	Indirect effects
Intrinsic motivation	.31	–	.24	.09
Self-regulation	.39	–	.24	.12
Computer competence	–	–	.44	–
Match	–	–	.58	–
Total effect (R^2)	.70		.79	

References

Anderson, T. (2003). Modes of interaction in distance education: Recent developments and research questions. In M. Moore (Ed.), *Handbook of distance education* (pp. 129–144). Mahwah: Lawrence Erlbaum.

Annand, D. (2011). Social presence within the community of inquiry framework. *International Review of Research in Open and Distance Learning, 12*(5), 40–56. Retrieved June 16, 2012 from http://www.irrodl.org/index.php/irrodl/article/view/924/1855.

Bernard, R. M., Abrami, P. C., Borokhovski, E., Wade, C. A., Tamim, R. M., Surkes, M. A., et al. (2009). A meta-analysis of three types of interaction treatments in distance education. *Review of Educational Research, 79*(3), 1243–1289.

Bogozzi, R. P., & Yi, Y. (1988). On the evaluation of structural equation models. *Journal of the Academy of Marketing Science, 16*(1), 74–94.

Branch, R. M. (1997). Educational technology frameworks that facilitate culturally pluralistic instruction. *Educational Technology, 37*(2), 38–41.

Collis, B. (1999). Designing for differences: Cultural issues in the design of WWW-based course-support sites. *British Journal of Educational Technology, 30*(3), 201–215.

Dabbagh, N. (2005). Pedagogical models for e-learning: A theory-based design framework. *International Journal of Technology in Teaching and Learning, 1*(1), 25–44.

Dillenbourg, P., Schneider, D., & Synteta, P. (2002). Virtual learning environments. In A. Dimitracopoulou (Ed.), *Proceedings of the 3rd Hellenic conference information & communication technologies in education*, pp. 3–18. Greece: Kastaniotis Editions.

Edmundson, A. (Ed.). (2007). *Globalized e-learning cultural challenges*. Hershey: Information Science Publishing.

Hannafin, M. J., & Land, S. (1997). The foundations and assumptions of technology-enhanced, student-centered learning environments. *Instructional Science, 25*, 167–202.

Henderson, L. (1996). Instructional design of interactive multimedia. *Educational Technology Research and Development, 44*(4), 85–104.

Jonassen, D. (1999). Designing constructivist learning environments. In C. M. Reigeluth (Ed.), *Instructional design theories and models: A new paradigm of instructional theory* (Vol. II, pp. 215–239). Mahwah: Lawrence Erlbaum Associates.

Jonassen, D. H., & Land, S. M. (2000). *Theoretical foundations of learning environments*. Mahwah: Lawrence Erlbaum Associates.

Ke, F. (2010). Examining online teaching, cognitive, and social presence for students. *Computers in Education, 55*(2), 808–820.

Ke, F. (2013). Online interaction arrangements on quality of online interactions performed by diverse learners across disciplines. *The Internet and Higher Education, 16*, 14–22.

Ke, F., & Kwak, D. (2013b). Constructs of student-centered online learning on learning satisfaction of a diverse online student body: A structural equation modeling approach. *Journal of Educational Computing Research, 48*(1), 97–122.

Lea, S. J., Stephenson, D., & Troy, J. (2003). Higher education students' attitudes to student-centred learning: Beyond 'educational bulimia'? *Studies in Higher Education, 28*(3), 321–334.

Macfadyen, L. P., Roche, J., Doff, S., Reeder, K., & Chase, M. (2004). *Communicating across cultures in cyberspace: A bibliographical review of intercultural communication online*. Piscataway: Transaction Publishers Distributor.

Marsh, H. W., Hau, K. T., & Wen, Z. (2004). In search of golden rules: Comment on hypothesis testing approaches to setting cutoff values for fit indexes and dangers in overgeneralizing Hu and Bentler's finding. *Structural Equations Modeling, 11*(3), 320–341.

McLoughlin, C., & Oliver, R. (2000). Designing learning environments for cultural inclusivity: A case study of Native American online learning at tertiary level. *Australian Journal of Educational Technology, 16*(1), 58–72.

Neumann, R., Parry, S., & Becher, T. (2002). Teaching and learning in their disciplinary contexts: A conceptual analysis. *Studies in Higher Education, 27*(4), 405–418.

Protheroe, N., & Turner, J. (2003). *Culturally sensitive instruction.* Arlington: Educational Research Service.

Rogers, P. C., Graham, C. R., & Mayes, C. T. (2007). Cultural competence and instructional design: Exploration research into the delivery of online instruction cross-culturally. *Educational Technology Research and Development, 55*(2), 197–217.

Swan, K. (2001). Virtual interaction: Design factors affecting student satisfaction and perceived learning in asynchronous online courses. *Distance Education, 22*(2), 306–331.

Walker, S. L., & Fraser, B. J. (2005). Development and validation of an instrument for assessing distance education learning environments in higher education: The Distance Education Learning Environments Survey (DELES). *Learning Environments Research, 8*(3), 289–308.

Part III
Designing for Success in Online Learning Contexts

Chapter 7
Inclusive Design of Online Teaching and Learning

In this chapter, we explore an adaptive and inclusive approach to instructional design for cross-cultural and intergenerational online learning. We start with a review and synthesis of existing instructional design propositions for culturally and age-related learning diversity and then provide a review and discussion of our project findings in relation to prior research. Based on the research findings as well as the literature, we advocate a participatory, fluid design process to select online instructional strategies for content, interface, activity, and technological infrastructure design.

Prior Online Instructional Design Propositions for Culture- and Age-Related Diversity

The earlier research on multicultural education in traditional classrooms proposed theories advocating incorporation of multiple cultures in instructional development. Frequently, these theories focused on K-12 school curriculum and teaching practice, described as "culturally responsive teaching" (Gay, 2000), "culturally relevant teaching" (Ladson-Billings, 1992), "culturally sensitive instruction" (Boyer, 1993), "multicultural instruction" (Saldana & Waxman, 1997), "culturally responsible pedagogy" (Pewewardy, 1994), or "equity pedagogy" (Banks & Banks, 1995). They emphasized the practice of multicultural education by the following: (1) providing pedagogical practices, contents, and learning activities that build on "the cultural knowledge, prior experiences, frames of reference, and performance styles" of culturally diverse students (Gay, 2000); (2) preparing students by developing their *cultural competence* and *awareness* (Ladson-Billings, 1992); (3) promoting culture-related equality as well as the appreciation of diversity (Banks & Banks, 1995; Boyer, 1993); and (4) creating bonds with and among students to develop collaborative learning. Empirical evidence has shown positive relation between those culturally responsive instructional theories and students' academic success

F. Ke and A.F. Chávez, *Web-Based Teaching and Learning across Culture and Age*,
DOI 10.1007/978-1-4614-0863-5_7, © Springer Science+Business Media New York 2013

(Gay, 2000). These theories or models for multicultural teaching in traditional classrooms provided useful frameworks for understanding and addressing issues of culture in web-based education settings.

The body of research on web-based teaching and learning contributes a variety of theoretical discussions and empirical descriptions of online instructional design models. Among them, Henderson's Multiple Cultures Theoretical Model (2007) (2007), developed based on Reeves and Reeves' (1997) Instructional Dimensions of Interactive Learning Environment, provides a representative framework that systematically and explicitly discusses culturally contextualized design for an online learning environment. Henderson (1996) classified culture-addressing instructional design perspectives into four approaches – inclusive, inverted curriculum approach, culturally unidimensional, and eclectic paradigm. The inclusive approach acknowledges multicultural realities but incorporates culture only in ways that have nothing to do with the content (e.g., inserting myths or pictures as fill-ins), composing *tokenism* or *stereotyping* in cultural representation. The inverted curriculum approach caters only to minority perspectives whereas culturally unidimensional approach only caters to dominant culture perspectives. Both fall short of supporting equity or inclusivity of multicultural needs, perspectives, contributions, or epistemologies. Henderson (1996) proposed an eclectic approach that endorses pedagogical representations of each culture in teaching/learning dimensions, flexibility in instructional design to cater for variability in usage, and multiplicity in epistemologies (e.g., behaviorist, constructivist, & social constructivist) for teaching and learning design. In particular, Henderson (2007) argued that a multicultural instructional design model should focus on the convention among learners' diverse cultural belongings, such as academic culture, ethnic culture, workplace culture, age, gender, religion, and class.

Henderson's works were further extended and investigated by McLoughlin and her colleagues (McLoughlin, 1999; McLoughlin & Oliver, 2000) during their examinations of the development of online learning environments for Indigenous learners in Australia. Adopting a social constructivist perspective, they advocated flexibility in adaptive course design and community-based collaborative learning.

Also adopting the flexibility norm, Collis, Vingerhoets, and Moonen (1997) outlined 19 pedagogical dimensions that could be adjusted dynamically in a technology-mediated course to address diverse learner needs. These pedagogical dimensions included those related to the content of the course, the expected prerequisites, instructional approach and resources, and course delivery and logistics.

Like Henderson (2007), Dillon, Wang, and Tearle (2007) argued that cultural connection or disconnection in online learning settings is more an interaction between multiple cultural dimensions, those of external (e.g., ethnic or national culture), internal (e.g., learners' age, gender, personality, and life experience), and academic (e.g., domain culture and instructional context). Given such a dynamic nature of cultural diversity, they then advocated that learners codesign with the instructor or instructional designer a culturally adaptive education environment.

Such a learner participatory design idea for culture-related e-learning development was also endorsed by Lin (2007).

Relevant to flexibility in online instruction is the integration and balance of multiplicity during design. In particular, Ibarra (2000) and Chávez (2007) argued that the learning environment must be designed to have good balance and integration of different cultural norms, such as high- and low-context cultural norms. Ramussen, Nichols, and Ferguson (2006), specifically, situated the discussion of multiculturalism in online education in a series of instructional strategies, such as orientation strategy, content strategy, interaction strategy, and conclusion or evaluation strategy.

Age can be considered a part of the cultural profile, and adult learning theories have been frequently cited during the discussion of culturally contextualized online learning development. However, there are few systematic discussions or empirical examinations focusing on age-related cultural inclusivity. Among the limited studies that focus on intergenerational or age-related online learning design (e.g., Cercone, 2008; Davis, 2006; Githens, 2007; Majeski & Stover, 2007; Patton, 2000; Sorensen & Murchú, 2004), flexibility in requirements, authentic activities and content development, and community-like collaborative learning design are three frequently proposed design principles.

Scholars typically theorized and prescribed a series of heuristic design principles for online adult learning. For example, Majeski and Stover (2007), based on the theory of significant learning (Fink, 2003), speculated a list of generic design suggestions for the development of the syllabus, presentation areas, discussion types, and group activities that are adult friendly in an online course setting. Those suggestions generally reflect the deep learning principles that are applicable for online students in general, such as providing immediacy to demonstrate teaching presence and to build an active learning community, providing individual feedback and support, and fostering active interactions. By synthesizing representative adult learning theories (i.e., andragogy, self-directed learning, experiential learning, and transformational learning), Cercone (2008) suggested that high-quality online learning for adults should be characterized by the following: (a) social interaction and collaboration with peers, (b) connecting new knowledge to past experience, (c) immediacy in application, (d) a climate of self-reflection, and (e) self-regulated learning. These theoretical papers laid out various conceptual propositions on adult-dominated online course design, but they provided only anecdotal evidence and there appears to be limited research available at present to support this evidence.

Discussion of Current Project Findings

Cultural and Intergenerational Diversity in Online Learning

The findings of the current research project suggest that we should take a critical view of the effect of ethnicity and age-related cultural differences within individual learners' online learning participation, interaction performance, and satisfaction. On one hand, there is no significant ethnicity-related difference in both reported and observed online peer-learning interaction participation and performance. There is not enough evidence supporting that learners of different ethnic roots would necessarily differ in interaction participation. Rather, individual learners' customs and performances of learning interaction varied dynamically, nurtured by a mixture of their general online learning conception, disciplinary or content domain, instructional design practice, and affordance of technology-mediated interaction platform.

It appears that the presence of culture during online interaction and learning is not a sturdy classification associated with one's ethnic or age group, but a manifestation of learners' prior and existing life, learning, and work contexts and involvements, which can be plural, adapted, and emergent. Such an observation is supported by the arguments of Dillon et al. (2007) that cultural disconnection in the online learning environment is the result of an interaction between outer culture characteristics (e.g., ethnic culture), inner culture characteristics (e.g., individual life experience and personality), and the educational environment (e.g., a specific instructional strategy and context). Gunawardena, Wilson, & Nolla (2003) stated that "researchers need to conceptualize identity issues in cross-cultural studies to go beyond simplistic stereotyping and use qualitative methods to understand how people define themselves" (p. 771). Such a statement can find support in our qualitative findings on the multiplicity and dynamic nature of cultural identities of online learners and instructors.

On the other hand, the project findings indicated a positive effect of age in online interaction participation. In particular, older learners posted more online discussion messages, spent more time in online learning activities, and reported a higher level of interaction participation. This finding is consistent with the report by Chyung (2007) that older students posted more often than younger students and the finding by Stafford and Lindsey (2007) that older, nontraditional students rated a web-based distant course higher for satisfaction than do their younger peers. It also supports the report by Wu and Teoh (2008) in a content analysis study of 1,451 online students' interaction transcripts. They found that older adults contributed to online discussions in more elaborate ways. Age-related cultural presence in this project appears to be associated with learners' experience, motivation, and prior learning custom, rather than age-related cognitive capabilities.

Notably, we found in our project that learners' ethnic status and their education background predict their perceived instructor support and performance of student-instructor interaction, with minority students and students of a higher educational background reporting higher levels of instructor support and student-instructor interaction. Additionally, minority students, compared with others, viewed or accessed online content folders more frequently. Such a finding was not explicitly mentioned in prior research. But Wang (2007) did report that national culture, such as power distance, would mediate online learners' perception of student-instructor interactions.

Minority students in this project reported less confidence and satisfaction with distance education in general, even though ethnicity does not predict learners' satisfaction toward specific online courses. The qualitative data suggested that learners of different ethnic roots can potentially adopt different cultural epistemologies toward learning (i.e., integrated vs. individuated) and hence develop different conceptions toward purpose of learning, ways of taking in and processing knowledge, interconnectedness of what is being learned, time, role of the teacher/control, student interactions, and sequencing. Native, Hispanic, Mestizo American, and perhaps other students of color in college are likely to reside firmly within an integrated cultural paradigm and practice in regard to learning. Further, it is likely with the Germanic and English origins of higher education and the high prevalence of faculty from cultures based within an individuated epistemology, many domestic and international students of color are experiencing a disconnect between their cultural ways of learning and learning experiences in college courses. Learners of minority status (e.g., Hispanic and Native American) could adapt themselves toward a potentially mismatched instructional context via more frequent student-instructor interactions or more time commitment for content absorption (e.g., content review or access). But they generally miss the personable presence of their instructors and the potential to build a bond with peers in online learning environments, which could decrease their comfort and satisfaction with distance education in general.

The aforementioned projection is consistent with previous works on the ethnic cultural trait of individualist and collectivist. For example, in a study of students' perceptions and preferences within a distance learning environment, Anakwe, Kessler, & Christensen (1999) surveyed 424 students, with a mean age of 25, 61 % being Caucasian, 14 % being Asian, 8 % being African American, 7 % being Hispanic, and 1 % being Native American. They reported that students of individualist ethnic culture origins prefer interactive medium and would consider distance learning for major course types, whereas students of collectivist ethnic culture (e.g., Hispanic and Native American) prefer face-to-face interactions and would consider distance learning for non-relationship course types. In agreement, Adams and Sean Evans (2004) as well as Smith and Ayers (2006) reported that in-person instruction and collaborative learning or learning community were the most appropriate and culturally respectful learning form for Navajo and Latino students (with a collectivist culture root).

Project findings also indicated learners' internal characteristics, such as their intrinsic motivation toward the learning subject and their self-regulation capability, positively mediate their perception on matching between learning preference and external online learning environments. Online learners reporting a match between learning preference and instructional context are more likely to report learning success and higher learning satisfaction. One implication of this finding is that a highly motivated and self-regulated learner may better adapt themselves toward the external online learning environment. It is consistent with a frequently reported claim by prior research that successful online learners often demonstrated a higher self-directed learning ability (Shinkareva & Benson, 2007).

At the same time, our qualitative findings indicate the prevalent acknowledgement of diversity, with a certain degree of appreciation or tolerance, from online learners across culture and age. A differing disposition toward cultural and age-related diversity, besides different levels of motivation and self-regulation, may be associated with learners' perception of their online learning experiences. As Parrish and Linder-Vanberschot (2010) argued, a positive disposition toward cultural diversity, demonstrated in different levels via acknowledgement, tolerance, respect, and appreciation, is a valuable asset for addressing the many challenges faced by the multicultural and intergenerational learner community. Multiple models on culturally responsive or relevant instruction (e.g., Gay, 2000; Ladson-Billings, 1992) have indicated the critical role of promoting both awareness and communication of diversity among learners and instructors. Therefore, it is valuable to include a purposeful and explicit element of cultural reflection and communication elements in online learning design and practice.

Cross-Cultural and Intergenerational Online Instruction

The aforementioned project findings imply that it is challenging, and even not meaningful, to simply seek or exploit static stereotypes on age- or ethnicity-related cultural diversity during online instructional design and practice. Instead, we should focus on exploring the salient online instruction that respects divergence and, more importantly, fosters cultural adaptation and multicultural versatility of online learners.

The project indicates that experiencing of personal relevance, authentic learning, active learning, and student autonomy will positively influence learners' satisfaction toward online courses and/or web-based education in general. It provides empirical evidence for the claim of prior research that an active, authentic, relevant, and student-centered online learning environment will promote learning satisfaction across culture and age (e.g., Dillenbourg, Schneider, & Synteta, 2002; Hannafin & Land, 1997, 2000).

In agreement with the prior research on multicultural instruction in traditional classrooms (e.g., Banks & Banks, 1995; Gay, 2000), this project highlights the potential of creating an *equity* learning environment that facilitates the knowledge construction process within learning interactions for students from diverse ethnic and age groups. The project finds that a balanced and inclusive design of three interaction mode arrangements (i.e., student-student, student-instructor, and student-content interactions) promotes knowledge-constructive and deep-learning-oriented learning interactions within online courses.

The project's qualitative findings indicate the instructional and learning benefits of understanding and analyzing the representation of integrative and individuated cultural constructs in diverse learners' knowledge construction process. Such a culturally analytic approach, as argued by scholars who proposed similar frameworks (e.g., Collis et al., 1997; Henderson, 1996; Parrish & Linder-VanBerschot, 2010), should assist instructors and designers seek a dynamic balance in all design and facilitative features of online courses, which is likely to lead to greatest satisfaction, persistence, and learning across culture and age.

Our qualitative findings imply that instructors with substantial (5+ years) online teaching experiences are willing to examine the participation patterns and learning needs of minority and nontraditional students. Yet during interviewing, few instructors would acknowledge or explicitly describe how their own cultural perspectives are represented in their instructional design decisions. Parrish and Linder-Vanberschot (2010) have argued that cultural sensitivity in online courses should not be just one way. Online education providers should become cognizant of the underlying mainstream cultures and the corresponding assumptions on teaching/learning and need to embrace the students' cultural and learning perspectives (Henderson, 1996). In this project, the instructors examined all reported a lack of training on online pedagogy and instructional design in general, not to mention the specific training on addressing culture- and age-related online learner diversity.

Inclusive Online Instructional Design

Protheroe and Turner (2003) warned that there won't be a single best teaching method to effectively address the cultural preferences of each and every student. We agree with Protheroe and Turner (2003) and other scholars that the purpose of culturally and intergenerational sensitive instruction is not to duplicate a learning environment based on a presumed cultural profile of each ethnic, age, academic major, or other related cultural group. Rather, the purpose is to build awareness and mutual accommodation for culture-related learner diversity during teaching and learning and promote cross-cultural and intergenerational adaptation to reach academic success.

In the following section, we describe four online instructional design principles that are extracted from our project findings and reflect major arguments of prior research on inclusive instructional design.

Fluid Instructional Design and Development

As observed in our study, it is common for online instructors to preplan all learning activities and materials beforehand, with little adaptation during the semester. However, it is challenging to prescribe and develop a culturally adaptive online learning environment before the actual occurrence and experience of learner diversity. As our project indicates, the presence or representation of culture- and age-related diversity in online learning often occurs from the dynamic interactions between learners' internal personalities or characteristics, their ethnicity- or age-related cultural perspectives, and the external academic context (e.g., the online course design).

As such, fluid development and customization of online instructional materials and activities throughout the semester, based on learners' input and performance, should be employed as an alternative to the prevalent practice of *predesign plus implementation as planned* for online instruction. Specifically, an online instructional provider, during the implementation process, should examine the assumptions they hold about how learners will and should respond to varied design decisions and then adjust those decisions based on the actual learner responses. An online instructor can construct a learning environment as an open-ended prototype and then keep concretizing or modifying its actual features and strategies through the academic semester. The degree of openness of such a design prototype can fluctuate along a continuum, via multiple dimensions (e.g., the content, learning tasks, technological tools, assessments). For example, an online instructor could provide a general content and activity timeline for online learners at the beginning, preplan 2–3 weeks' learning activities and materials, and then adaptively develop the remaining learning modules based on the emerging learner responses and needs.

Moreover, the fluid instructional design and development process can build on the interaction with targeted students or student representatives during the design, implementation, and evaluation phases. It can reflect the principle of participatory design (Schuler & Namioka, 1993) by incorporating user- (or learner-) generated content and strategies.

Dual Responsibility: Acculturation and Accommodation

This current project suggests that online instructors and students, especially those with plural cultural roots, experience of guest culture exposure, or training with cultural awareness and respect, are likely to report a positive disposition toward learner diversity and perform cross-cultural adaptation during teaching and learning interactions. Self-regulated and intrinsically motivated learners also tend to better adapt themselves to the external academic culture. Students of minority groups have demonstrated similar participation and performance levels during online learning interactions as their peers. An equivalent performance may encompass minority students' effort of cultural adaptation to the main stream culture represented by the online course context.

An implication of the aforementioned project findings is the need to foster acculturation in a diversity-sensitive online learning environment – enabling the development and performance of mutual cross-cultural adaptation during online teaching and learning. Consistent with prior research, this project suggests that online instructors and students are adaptable and culture can be learned. "Teaching and learning are not only embedded in culture, they are cultural transmission in action – the means to culture" (Parrish & Linder-VanBerschot, 2010, p. 5).

Therefore, inclusive online education should serve the dual responsibilities of acculturation (i.e., promoting cultural versatility for the sake of promoting learning) and accommodation (i.e., being adaptive to learners' diversity). Acculturation can start from the practice of critical reflection, explicit communication, and the development of awareness of and respect for diverse culture-related differences and preferences. For example, explicit cross-cultural interaction norms can be purposefully communicated and negotiated during an online course. Direct instruction, explanation, or sharing of desirable learning and teaching conceptions and strategies should also be encouraged. Another component of acculturation is to perform a critical analysis to understand what learning preferences and behaviors are "based on deeply entrenched cultural values" and hence need greater accommodation (Parrish & Linder-VanBerschot, 2010, p. 10) and what preferences and behaviors are more prone to be modified or acculturated to serve the learning and instructional goals.

Accommodation can be provided by integrating the diversity of learners' cultural characteristics into the content (e.g., content objects) and the knowledge construction process (e.g., learning interactions, online instructional activities, and assessments) during online instructional design. More discussions on the practice of accommodation are presented in the following two subsections.

Balanced Arrangement of Interaction Modes

In this project, a balanced arrangement of student-content, student-student, and student-instructor interactions appears to promote the most learning participation and satisfaction for learners across ethnicity, age, and academic discipline. An integrative and balanced arrangement of the three interaction modes can be viewed as an online instructional design practice that enables the presence of *multiplicity* in teaching and learning epistemologies (Henderson, 2007; Reeves & Reeves, 1997). A comparable requirement of learners' participation and performance of different types of learning interactions will help learners of diverse preferences and styles to find a preferred mode of knowledge construction (e.g., via solitary reading, peer discussion, or comprehending instruction) while having the chance to stretch themselves beyond the comfort zone. It also helps to create the most comprehensive existence of teaching presence, cognitive presence, and social presence, the three essential components of a successful online learning environment (Garrison, Anderson, & Archer, 2000; Ke, 2010).

Multiplicity and Flexibility in Online Instructional Design and Practice

As the project indicates, online learners are likely to have a diversity of individual- or cultural-group-related preferences, conceptions, and customs for learning and interaction participation. To create a culturally versatile or inclusive learning setting, embedding multiplicity in the arrangement of learning interactions and the selection of platforms for learning interactions is critical. Giving alternatives as to the content, requirement, task, and activity structure of knowledge construction (i.e., learning interactions in this project) should foster learning and satisfaction of online learners, especially that of nontraditional students.

Student-Content Interaction Design

The project indicated student-content interaction as a foundational component of all three learning interactions. Online learners, across ethnicity, age, and academic fields, value the diversity and multiplicity in the content objects (e.g., reading, lecturing presentation, video/audio clips, cases), tasks for the sake of content processing (e.g., individual or group, project or exam, paper or presentation), and content presentation formats (e.g., multimodal and multimedia messages). Particularly, adult learners appear to prefer content objects with a presence of simplicity (e.g., easy to find and process) and learning tasks with an open-ended or flexible requirement (e.g., a flexible deadlines). Although Henderson (1996) deemed the inclusion of non-content-related cultural messages as a superficial *cultural token*, our project findings indicated that embedding student-culture- and academic-topic-themed visuals in the interface of the online course site can improve the social presence of the online learning environment. As our online learners reported, an interface-based cultural token is valuable by indicating the instructor's cultural awareness and his or her expectation to foster a positive cultural disposition in the online learning setting.

Student-Instructor Interaction Design

The web-based student-instructor interaction, as our project indicates, comprises multiple processes (e.g., learner management, virtual lecturing, facilitation, and learner support), multiple dimensions (e.g., academic vs. social), and multiple tools or platforms (e.g., asynchronous e-mail, grading feedback, announcement, online discussion post, and synchronous scaffolding/lecturing via text chat and web conferencing). Instructors examined in this project played a variety of roles during interaction (e.g., a monitor, leader, and facilitator) and taken on different types of presence (e.g., personable vs. "shadowy," academic vs. social, supportive vs. challenging).

The selection among the spectrum of diverse processes, representations, and the tools of the student-instructor interaction is a critical instructional design decision. As proposed by prior research and supported by the project findings, online instructional design should arrange for multiple strategies and technologies to deliver the student-instructor interaction, with a dynamic, localized fluctuation in the spectrum of low to high, student-initiated to instructor-initiated interactions.

The localized fluctuation can be based on the observation of teaching and learning needs in different online courses, different course modules, and different learner groups.

Student-Student Interaction Design

Although the student-student interaction was adopted as the major online learning activity in most online courses, online learners demonstrated different levels of participation and different dispositions toward student-student interactions. The diversity is mediated by learners' internal learning conceptions, the discipline culture, and the external instructional contexts more than by their ethnicity- or age-related backgrounds. Since not all online learners view peer interaction as a necessary component of learning, it is critical to design an interaction task that justifies or necessitates collaborative knowledge construction, rather than designing a discussion for the discussion sake. It is also important to plan a compound of purposes (e.g., reading comprehension vs. collaborative case analysis or solution exploration), activity structures (e.g., in group or class), and appraisal criterion for the student-student interaction in order to address learner diversity. The selection of types and levels of student-student interaction (e.g., social, reading oriented, or assignment centered), its platform (e.g., discussion forum vs. web conferencing), and activity structure, again, does not need to be standardized across online programs, courses, or even course modules. The selection should be dynamically made and changed based on an observation and analysis of the emergent online learning behaviors and responses during the implementation phase.

References

Adams, T., & Sean Evans, R. (2004). Educating the educators: Outreach to the college of education distance faculty and Native American Students. *Journal of Library Administration, 41*(1/2), 3–18.

Anakwe, U. P., Kessler, E. H., & Christensen, E. W. (1999). Distance learning and cultural diversity: Potential users' perspective. *International Journal of Organizational Analysis, 7*(3), 224–243.

Banks, C. A. M., & Banks, J. A. (1995). Equity pedagogy: An essential component of multicultural education. *Theory into Practice, 34*(3), 152–158.

Boyer, J. B. (1993). Culturally sensitive instruction: An essential component of education for diversity. *Catalyst for Change, 22*(3), 5–8.

Cercone, K. (2008). Characteristics of adult learners with implications for online learning design. *AACE Journal, 16*(2), 137–159.

Chávez, A. F. (2007). Islands of empowerment: Facilitating multicultural learning communities in college. *International Journal of Teaching and Learning in Higher Education, 19*(3), 274–288.

Chyung, S. (2007). Age and gender differences in online behavior, self-efficacy, and academic performance. *Quarterly Review of Distance Education, 8*(3), 213–222. Retrieved March 29, 2009, from Education Research Complete database.

Collis, B., Moonen, J., & Vingerhoets, J. (1997). Flexibility as a key construct in European training: Experiences from the TeleScopia project. *British Journal of Educational Technology, 28*(3), 199–217.

Davis, J. (2006). Designing an online course for nontraditional students: Revisiting the essentials. *International Journal of Learning, 12*(10), 121–127.

Dillenbourg, P., Schneider, D., & Synteta, P. (2002). Virtual learning environments. In A. Dimitracopoulou (Ed.), *Proceedings of the 3rd Hellenic conference information & communication technologies in education*, pp. 3–18. Greece: Kastaniotis Editions.

Dillon, P., Wang, R., & Tearle, P. (2007). Cultural disconnection in virtual education. *Pedagogy, Culture & Society, 15*(2), 153–174. Retrieved March 29, 2009, doi:10.1080/14681360701403565.

Fink, L. D. (2003). *Creating significant learning experiences: An integrated approach to designing college courses*. San Francisco: Jossey Bass.

Garrison, D. R., Anderson, T., & Archer, W. (2000). Critical inquiry in a text-based environment: Computer conferencing in higher education. *The Internet and Higher Education, 2*(2–3), 87–105.

Gay, G. (2000). *Culturally responsive teaching: Theory, research, & practice*. New York: Teachers College Press.

Githens, R. P. (2007). Older adults and e-learning: Opportunities and barriers. *The Quarterly Review of Distance Education, 8*(4), 329–338.

Gunawardena, C., Wilson, P., & Nolla, A. (2003). Culture and online education. In M. Morre & W. Anderson (Eds.), *Handbook of distance education* (pp. 753–775). Mahwah: Lawrence Erlbaum.

Hannafin, M. J., & Land, S. (1997). The foundations and assumptions of technology-enhanced, student-centered learning environments. *Instructional Science, 25*, 167–202.

Hannafin, M. J., & Land, S. M. (2000). Technology and student-centered learning in higher education: Issues and practices. *Journal of Computing in Higher Education, 12*(1), 3–30.

Henderson, L. (1996). Instructional design of interactive multimedia. *Educational Technology Research and Development, 44*(4), 85–104.

Henderson, L. (2007). Theorizing a multiple cultures instructional design model for e-learning and e-teaching. In A. Edmundson (Ed.), *Globalized e-learning cultural challenges* (pp. 130–153). Hershey, PA: Idea Group Inc.

Ibarra, R. (2000). Studying Latinos in a "Virtual" University: Reframing diversity and academic culture change. Occasional Paper No. 68. Latino studies series. East Lansing: Julian Samora Research Institute. Retrieved March 31, 2009, from ERIC database.

Ke, F. (2010). Examining online teaching, cognitive, and social presence for adult students. *Computers in Education, 55*(2), 808–820.

Ladson-Billings, G. (1992). Culturally relevant teaching: The key to making multicultural education work. In C. A. Grant (Ed.), *Research and multicultural education* (pp. 106–121). London: Falmer Press.

Lin, C. (2007). e-Learning strategies for aboriginal children in Taiwan. *International Journal of Learning, 14*(6), 153–160. Retrieved April 29, 2009, from Education Research Complete database.

Majeski, R., & Stover, M. (2007). Theoretically based pedagogical strategies leading to deep learning in asynchronous online gerontology courses. *Educational Gerontology, 33*(3), 171–185.

McLoughlin, C. (1999). Culturally responsive technology use: Developing an on-line community of learners. *British Journal of Educational Technology, 30*(3), 231–243.

McLoughlin, C., & Oliver, R. (2000). Designing learning environments for cultural inclusivity: A case study of Native American online learning at tertiary level. *Australian Journal of Educational Technology, 16*(1), 58–72.

Parrish, P., & Linder-VanBerschot, J. A. (2010). Cultural dimensions of learning: Addressing the challenges of multicultural instruction. *International Review of Research in Open and Distance Learning, 11*(2), 1–19.

Patton, M. (2000). The importance of being flexible with assignment deadlines. *Higher Education in Europe, 25*(3), 417–423.

Pewewardy, C. D. (1994). Culturally responsible pedagogy in action: An American Indian magnet school. In E. R. Hollins, J. E. King, & W. C. Haymon (Eds.), *Teaching diverse populations: Formulating a knowledge base* (pp. 77–92). Buffalo: State University of New York Press.

Protheroe, N., & Turner, J. (2003). *Culturally sensitive instruction*. Arlington: Educational Research Service.

Rasmussen, K., Nichols, J., & Ferguson, F. (2006). It's a new world: Multiculturalism in a virtual environment. *Distance Education, 27*(2), 265–278. Retrieved March 29, 2009, doi:10.1080/01587910600789696.

Reeves, T., & Reeves, P. (1997). Effective dimensions of interactive learning on the world wide web. In B. Khan (Ed.), *Web-based instruction* (pp. 59–66). Englewood Cliffs: Educational Technology Publications.

Saldana, D. C., & Waxman, H. C. (1997). An observational study of multicultural education in urban elementary schools. *Equity and Excellence in Education, 30*(1), 40–46.

Schuler, D., & Namioka, A. (Eds.). (1993). *Participatory design: Principles and practices*. Hillsdale: Lawrence Erlbaum Associates.

Shinkareva, O., & Benson, A. (2007). The relationship between adult students' instructional technology competency and self-directed learning ability in an online course. *Human Resource Development International, 10*(4), 417–435.

Smith, D., & Ayers, D. (2006). Culturally responsive pedagogy and online learning: Implications for the globalized community college. *Community College Journal of Research & Practice, 30*(5/6), 401–415.

Sorensen, E., & Murchú, D. (2004). Designing online learning communities of practice: A democratic perspective. *Journal of Educational Media, 29*(3), 189–200.

Stafford, T., & Lindsey, K. (2007). IP teleconferencing in the wired classroom: Gratifications for distance education. *Journal of Information Systems Education, 18*(2), 227–232.

Wang, M. (2007). Designing online courses that effectively engage learners from diverse cultural backgrounds. *British Journal of Educational Technology, 38*(2), 294–311.

Wu, B., & Teoh, P. A. (2008). A comparative analysis of learners interaction in the online learning management systems: Does national culture matter? *Asian Association of Open Universities Journal, 3*(1), 1–16.

Chapter 8
Promoting Inclusive, Deep Learning in Online Contexts

Developing the design, climate, social, and academic presence of instructors and students, as well as pedagogical activities both online and outside the web-based learning context, is a complex endeavor. This complexity and flexibility is necessary to developing an inclusive learning culture in web-based instructional contexts. We encourage faculty to start with simple formats and develop course complexity over time. Partnering with students, especially those from different cultures than the instructors own, is essential to this development.

Key Considerations in Developing Inclusive Online Learning Cultures

It is helpful for instructors to consider some principles or considerations that differ fundamentally from teaching in a face-to-face context. Over time, it becomes clear to many instructors that to develop deep learning experiences for and with students in web-based contexts, it is necessary to work from a different set of understandings. This can be a bit uncomfortable at first, perhaps like shifting from riding a bicycle to riding a horse. Good teaching in either a face-to-face or web-based context requires partnering with students, focusing on their learning more than on our teaching, and moving flexibly within the learning context. Yet in an online course, students seem more likely to "take off on their own" even when the instructor is highly involved and paying close attention. Once an instructor gets used to this, it can be a powerful instructional dynamic. Some key considerations when designing and facilitating web-based courses include the following.

F. Ke and A.F. Chávez, *Web-Based Teaching and Learning across Culture and Age*,
DOI 10.1007/978-1-4614-0863-5_8,

The Instructor Is Not the Primary Focus of Student Attention

With the exception of intermittent queries to the instructor for clarifications, students' primary focus within a web-based learning context is mostly on the content of the course, their own learning, and if designed accordingly, on their interactions with each other. In essence, web-based instructors must develop a kind of "egoless" sense of teaching, knowing that much of their role is as a behind the scenes learning designer, guide, and facilitator. The positive aspect of this reality is that focus is placed firmly on students and student learning. Even when faculty offer videotaped lectures or facilitate online class sessions, students seem to be less focused on faculty at the center of their learning than in face-to-face courses. This can be a bit disconcerting for some faculty who are used to and perhaps enjoy this dynamic in a face-to-face course. Some faculty will find this more comfortable while others find it less. Either way, it is a significant adjustment in conceptualizing learning design and facilitation.

An Active Caring Presence Is Key to Student Learning, Satisfaction, and Success

Even though instructors are not the primary focus of student attention in a web-based course, faculty social and academic presence is a critical factor in student learning, satisfaction, and success. Students, especially from more integrated cultures, benefit from instructors who overtly indicate their dedication to students through responsiveness to student queries and needs, complex design, and positive, encouraging interactions with students. There are many ways faculty can show an active and caring presence including responding quickly to e-mails and other kinds of student queries, joining in online discussions, developing an online course design that is "user-friendly" in part based on ongoing student input, offering a variety of kinds of learning experiences and assignments based in differing ways students learn, and finding ways to connect as human beings to students through sharing of professional and/or personal stories.

A Variety of Learning Experiences to Match a Diversity of Student Ways of Learning

Students learn and are most satisfied and successful in web-based courses that at least in some ways match their own natural or preferred ways of learning. Because any one web-based course has a variety of student learners, it is beneficial to develop courses that are inclusive of many ways of learning and doing. Students benefit most when a variety of assignment and evaluation types, online activities, connections to real-life situations or case studies, ways of reflecting and interacting, and ways of disseminating knowledge are used over time within a course. For example, if all assignments are written or evaluations happen only through tests, certain types of learners (verbal and logical) have their ways of learning/doing privileged throughout the course, while others (such as visual or kinesthetic learners) do not. Over time, instructors can purposefully develop a wider variety of ways of presenting materials, facilitating interactions, and sequencing learning components. It can be very helpful to apply a culture- or diversity-related learning model such as the Cultural Constructs Teaching and Learning Model in Chap. 5 (Fig. 5.2) to consider and design a variety of types of learning activities.

Shaping an Integrative Cultural Epistemology of Teaching

Native, Hispano, and Mestizo American college students in this study reside firmly within an integrated cultural epistemology in regard to learning. It is likely that within the Germanic and English cultural origins of higher education and high prevalence of faculty from cultures based in these individuated cultural epistemologies, many domestic and international students of color are experiencing a disconnect between their own cultural epistemologies of learning and learning processes experienced in college courses (Brayboy & Maughan, 2009; Guido-DiBrito & Chávez, 2003; Ibarra, 2001; Rendón, 2009).

In most ways, integrated cultural epistemologies of learning were quite similar for Native, Hispano, and Mestizo students in this study. Students described their preferred learning processes as interconnected, contextual, involving mind/body/spirit/emotions, starting with doing/examples/storytelling, including broader conceptions of time and built-in ways to learn with and from peers, involving feeling cared about by the professor, and incorporating metaphorical and symbolic representations of course content.

There were some distinctive differences in how aspects of integrated epistemologies played out for Native and Hispano students. Native American students spoke of the importance of professors providing archival/historical ways to return to earlier course content, time for individual and collective reflection, visual means of learning, and learning from other students especially by reviewing their assignments:

> Brayboy and Maughan (2009) suggest that Native American peoples "…come to know things by living their lives and adding to a set of cumulative experiences that serve as guideposts for both individuals and communities over time. In other words, individuals live and enact their knowledge and, in the process, engage further in the process" (pp. 3–4).

To enhance learning and success across cultural epistemologies of students, we would encourage faculty to assess their own cultural constructs of learning and systematically observe how these cultural epistemologies play out in current pedagogy; relational dynamics with students; assumptions we make about students, education, and learning; and classroom climate. Faculty who teach might consider blending some of the suggestions for integrated cultural constructs of teaching and learning, not already present, into their teaching to shape more culturally inclusive learning contexts with and for students who abide within integrated epistemologies of learning. We believe this would be beneficial to student learning among Native, Hispano, and Mestizo students as well as students from other integrated cultural origins. Though faculty from minority and mixed cultural origins in our study were more likely to include a mix of cultural epistemologies in their design, it can be a reverse challenge for some faculty to design from within their own integrated forms of teaching and learning to balance with individuated forms of pedagogy, interactions, and climate. Once again, applying the missing side or components of the cultural constructs model and other models can be very helpful in developing an inclusive learning culture online.

Find Ways to Overtly Show Care for Students

Integrated learners are situated within a highly relational cultural epistemology and often expect overt expressions of care from those around them. These students are likely to learn most effectively when they feel cared about by professors. If professors are comfortable, they can share stories of themselves in relation to the subject. Advising and office hours can be used to assist students with academic needs as well as show care. Hispano, Mestizo, and Native students are likely to interweave questions about academics with sharing about relationships, life struggles, etc. These connections are made for integrated learners as a natural part of communicating within an integrated worldview. This sharing may include spiritual, familial, tribal, financial, and health-related aspects affecting their education. Listening and referring students to appropriate campus offices is often enough to show care to students and encourage them to continue in their academics. Faculty can add a continuing practice to their teaching by taking a few moments in classes or in weekly messages/announcements throughout the semester to highlight various campus services which takes little time and goes a long way in communicating care to students. Providing information about services on campus to assist students with the many parts of their lives such as childcare, student counseling, recreational services, tutoring, and financial aid is a technique that allows faculty to signal empathy for students by acknowledging the realities of their lives while referring students to professionals on campus who are available to assist in these areas.

Offer Contextual Connections of Course Content Across Mind, Body, Spirit, and Emotions

Integrated learners feel a need to connect academic content to self, family, tribe, community, and the natural world as essential to their learning. This is often most helpful prior to processing abstract or theoretical components of the subject because it brings learning first into personal context for integrated learners. Most students in this study shared that their professors almost never related academic subjects beyond an abstract, mind-oriented context to student home communities or their own lives and expressed concern about this as an oversight of teaching. Finding ways to make connections between academic subject areas and student lives is unique to each professor and course. Some professors may feel comfortable adding their own stories and examples of connections between themselves and academic content, discussing challenges they have faced in learning or offering examples of application in their professional experiences. Faculty may also consider facilitating connections between course content and aspects of students' lives. Some students in this study described projects or examples that helped them make connections to their own lives. One Native American student described a chemistry professor who had them collect soil samples from old mining sites on tribal lands to test toxicity and then discussed the implications for the health and well-being of tribal peoples, plant life, and wildlife in these areas. A Hispano American student described a nursing professor who had them develop health charts of their families and in their communities to assess health-care needs and patterns. A mechanical engineering professor discussed ways he moved away from what he described as an "engineering culture of teaching" that always starts with the abstract toward alternating sometimes starting with a real situation (such as a cup falling over or water system needs in rural area of South America) and processing toward abstract theory while other times starting with the traditional abstract theory to practice normative in the field. This professor described his pleasant surprise at how much better this worked in assisting all students to learn and to feel comfortable with and understand connections of theory and practice.

Learners from integrated cultural epistemological origins are likely to expect to explore knowledge through the mind, body, spirit, and emotions. These students may feel lost or limited if learning does not go beyond mind-only exploration. Instructors are encouraged to incorporate a variety of lenses and processes in learning throughout assignments, class activities, and interactions with students. Simply asking how students feel about what they are learning and exploring implications of what they are learning to their own lives and communities can often lead to these important connections for students. Often, the more abstract the discipline or subject, the more fear or discomfort students with origins in an integrated epistemology/worldview feel in learning. Instructor facilitation of discussions about what makes this uncomfortable or even frightening can lead to helpful understandings of the discipline or theory itself. Instructors who facilitate these kinds of conversations with students in classes often discover key components and dynamics that students are missing or not understanding and are able to develop instructional processes to enhance learning more effectively over time.

Incorporate a Variety of Integrated Pedagogical Elements: Questions of Time and Process

Students in this study often spoke of learning through visual and other nonverbal means and found it helpful when teachers used models, charts, drawings, symbols, and other visual representations to explain concepts. Most found it difficult to learn when teaching consisted of only words in visual and audio forms. Instructors are encouraged over time to include visual aspects beyond words to enhance learning for all. Video, websites, student crafted objects, models, charts, photographs, art, and other visual images can assist in offering students more than one way to explore and understand a specific concept. Many integrated learners in this study also spoke of their use of metaphor or symbol as part of their process of making sense of what they were learning. Faculty can facilitate this type of processing among students by asking students to reflect between class sessions on a metaphor or representation of an idea, concept, or process and be ready to discuss or share in the next class. One of the authors for this book regularly has students in research courses describe and compare qualitative and quantitative research modes of inquiry through the use of metaphor, drawings, music, and poetry. The more abstract the concept, the more a variety of learning processes are essential to integrated learners. Even the act of having to figure things out enhances learning as does hearing from other students both about how they interpret or make sense of a theory or concept and about the process they went through to journey to this understanding.

Many integrated learners benefit from time to reflect on questions they might have for the instructor, time to think about a question asked by the instructor prior to having to respond, and time to reflect before class discussions. Even a moment can give students time to pull together a few thoughts, jot down notes, or sketch an idea. Online written discussions which often take place over a period of days in a web-based course facilitate this reflection naturally.

In online class sessions, faculty can offer a moment for students to jot down ideas prior to asking for input or pose questions for discussion prior to class time. Native American students often grow up in cultural environs where contemplation and reflection are a large part of everyday life (Covarrubias & Windchief, 2009). One Mestiza author's mother often encouraged her children to "go out and sit by the river and think about life" and found it difficult in formal educational contexts to respond without first being allowed quiet time to reflect. Instructors can also acknowledge this need in some learners by purposefully protecting time for reflection and encouraging external processors not to chat during these silent times. It can be very helpful to alternate time for reflection with time for immediate discussion so that internal and external processors benefit from both kinds of interactions.

Offering a variety of forms of evaluation is important to varying student conceptions of time and ways of thinking and learning. Timed tests may have disproportional effect on students from differing cultural backgrounds. Native, Hispano, and Mestizo students in this study spoke of the importance of time to reflect, sleep, dream, pray, and meditate to process effectively and suggested that professors have some timed and some take-home tests to create a more culturally inclusive balance of time in evaluation processes.

Offering choices in format for assignments and projects naturally facilitates a variety of ways students make sense of knowledge. Moving from always requiring a paper or exam for example to offering options for students to respond to an assignment in other formats such as PowerPoints, e-posters, website developments, and video offers venues to incorporate many ways of presenting knowledge and increases complexity of many assignments. Asking students to share and discuss their own and others' projects online typically increases the caliber of projects and increases student learning by offering many ways to explore a concept or topic across a group of learners in a class. Over the course of a semester or quarter, students could be asked to do several different types of evaluative learning components (e.g., a paper, an exam, and a project presentation).

Learn from Each Other

Many integrated learners, especially among Hispanic students in this research project, spoke of a wish to learn from student peers through discussion, group activities, and reviewing peer assignments. This was explained as a process of comparing and contrasting their ideas with others bringing clarity to thinking. Many also spoke of their own feelings of responsibility to assisting other students to learn. Faculty can incorporate group processing activities in class to assist students in figuring out complex concepts, solving a problem, creating a solution, or processing a case study. In addition, online library e-reserves, web enhancement of courses, and other means can be applied to allow students to access each other's assignments for peer review, as readings for the class, or to share parts of an evolving group assignment.

One faculty member regularly has at least one set of student assignments become readings for the entire class by letting students know their projects/papers will be shared as a class reading and then uploading them after the due date to the course site. This faculty member and students in the class have remarked that sharing assignments increased the quality of student work; allowed everyone to learn from student efforts, insights, and thought; widened the diversity of knowledge accessible by class members; built self-esteem among individual students; and increased appreciation of peer knowledge.

Online asynchronous and synchronous discussions are another way to enhance knowledge and experience sharing among students in web-based courses. As noted earlier, written discussions allow more reflective, internal processing students the time to prepare and interact deeply with peers. Synchronous discussions in both written and audio forms may be more conducive to peer learning and processing among external processing students who benefit from immediate responses. Alternating synchronous and asynchronous discussions is likely to improve learning among all students. In many of the beginning math courses in this study, students were required to work online in discussion groups on problems and writing with the stated directive for students to work together during the week until everyone understood and could demonstrate math concepts. Students were charged with making sure their peers understood concepts throughout the semester. Since teaching others is an excellent way to increase one's own understanding, this learning technique enhances learning for everyone in a class.

Engage the Power of the Internet and Student Lives in the Learning Process

Web-based courses offer a unique opportunity and openness for connecting students to the world outside a specific course or collegiate institution. We encourage faculty to make use of available resources via the Internet in the form of links, educational tools and assessments, professionals' sites, and even social media. One astronomy professor in this study created a highly complex course complete with links to publicly available observatory sites around the world, astronomical charts, calculation tools, and star/planet gazing real-time observation links. Another professor, realizing the highly rural nature of her students, asked her students to suggest ways they might interact more effectively and began to have students upload discussion thoughts to a shared Twitter site from their cell phones. Some faculty in the study connected subject matter to student home communities by asking students regularly to make connections as well as having students develop community-based projects, papers, and research.

Design and Instructional Techniques for an Inclusive Online Learning Context

In this section, we would like to discuss specific design and instructional techniques for constructing an inclusive online instructional context. These techniques are both data-driven by the project findings on the learning or instructional contexts of the online courses examined and model-driven syntheses of prior research on e-learning design and our Online Instructional Context framework presented in Chap. 6.

Direct and Indirect Teaching Presence

It is typical for a designer or an instructor to plan and organize a traditional education experience via a series of instructional events, following a chronological order. Such an event-centered, time-sequenced teaching practice is challenged by the asynchronous nature of the online education setting. Moreover, the traditional approach of teaching via "stand-up presentation" and "hands-on mentoring" is difficult online. As such, the center of direct learning interaction, as observed in this project, seems to shift from an instructor (or trainer) in a traditional learning setting (as a sage on the stage or a guide on the side) to the *content* (information to be delivered) in an online setting. In all online courses examined, student-content interaction, or the design and presentation of the materials via diverse types of content objects, constitutes the most foundational element of the learning environment design. Actually, it is unusual that a novice instructor will simply upload all lecturing and practice materials online and expect students to mainly learn by reading. Although some scholars have argued that high-quality content-student interaction can possibly replace content-instructor interaction (Anderson, 2003), our project findings indicate certain learner groups still need and value the personable, social presence of teaching and expect direct interaction with an instructor.

In this section, we propose three design solutions for constructing direct and indirect teaching presence (i.e., student-instructor interaction) in an online learning setting: (1) constructing both interactive and noninteractive teaching presence, (2) providing both individualized and protocolized learner management and support, and (3) projecting social, personable identity of the instructor into the course interface and communication.

Interactive and Noninteractive Teaching Presence

As observed, online instructors can integrate their direct instruction into the content objects to be distributed. They do so by videotaping face-to-face lecturing process and putting the video clips online as the learning materials. Some also create lecturing slides with voice-over explanation or podcasts with instructional narration. These lecturing materials, though noninteractive, manage to convey the academic presence of online instructors. In other terms, the student-content interaction process in the online learning setting is blended with the student-instructor interaction. Other instructors choose to construct more interactive teaching presence via text-based posts (e.g., creating a "virtual office" via discussion board or blog) and/or web conferencing. The interactive teaching presence can be conveyed across distance via text-, audio-, video-, and even 3D virtual-reality-based lecturing and mentoring.

Individualized and Protocolized Learner Management and Support

Individual support and learner management are especially challenging while highly sought in the online setting. Text-based asynchronous feedback for each student, via assignment grading and post commenting, is the most often observed learner support. The assignment feedback is not necessarily written and can be provided via adaptive audio comments (e.g., audio comments via the Adobe Professional or podcasting). Some instructors will also check the online activity log and other participation profiles to identify less engaged students and send each of them an individual e-mail.

The aforementioned learner management or support techniques, however, are not prompt and can be time and effort consuming. Online instructors may also provide individual help by phone and scheduled text chat or web conferencing. Still, adaptive synchronous support is rarely occurring mainly due to the differing, busy schedules of both instructor and online learners (with most of them part-time, non-traditional students). As such, a protocolized practice of learner management and support can be planned as a complement. For example, semester-long or weekly advanced organizers, in a calendar view, can be presented and highlighted on the course website. Daily or weekly announcements can be posted and e-mailed to summarize the learning progress and remind students of major activities or events. In our project, a group of online instructors set up a "virtual-office" discussion forum and let students know that they would daily check this discussion forum to answer questions. This virtual office has been frequently mentioned and praised by their students.

Projection of a Personable Identity

Study findings indicated that a personable social presence of the online instructor helps to reinforce online learning satisfaction. Online instructors should take every chance to project their social presence and personable identity into the course content, the interface design, and daily student-instructional interactions. Instructors can share their personal experiences, stories, and perspectives within the learning materials and online posts to create more social presence. We also found that online courses with a personalized, visual-rich interface (e.g., comprising pictorial icons and content-topic-related image banners), in comparison to those with the default text-tense and file-folder-themed standard view, receive more positive reactions from students across ethnic and age groups. The instructor should also be mindful of the *netiquette* in e-mails, posts, and other written communications (e.g., greeting and addressing names, inserting smiley icons; Shea, 1994).

Efficiency of Online Facilitation

Online interaction and learning facilitation is found to be an essential element of online instruction. In our project, online instructors differ in their participation level: Some dominate or lead the interaction, some are guides on the side, and others are only monitoring. Their facilitation also differs in the timing: Some tend to only initiate the discussion and some will wait until the end to synthesize or wrap up the discussion, while others will participate all through the session. There are also multiple approaches to online facilitation: Some focus on appraising, some tend to post probes or inquiries, and some serve as experts who elaborate and explain concepts or synthesize across differing perspectives to provide a conclusion. Online instructors are using online interaction spaces as an instructional "microworld" to implement their teaching epistemologies and experiment with their regular teaching techniques. Our suggestion, as discussed in the previous chapter, is to provide multiplicity in the online facilitating practice and adapt the techniques dynamically based on learners' reactions during the semester.

Investment Analysis with Facilitation Techniques

Online facilitation, at the same time, is the most frequently mentioned time-consuming element of online instruction. An efficient practice of online facilitation involves a time or investment appraisal of diverse approaches or alternatives that serve the same design or instructional purpose. Like the needs and learner analysis, a time or investment analysis with a variety of viable online instructional techniques should be considered a component of the design analysis. This analysis process can be associated with the aforementioned cultural analysis. The technique chosen should be the one that is relatively efficient while not sacrificing its being learner adaptive (i.e., by addressing the learning preferences or needs that are based on entrenched cultural backgrounds and hence hard to challenge).

Orientation and User-Friendly Information Design

Other instructional practices that improve the efficiency of online facilitation include providing a good orientation at the beginning of the semester on the expected online learning process and increasing the usability of the online learning environment. Both practices will prepare online learners, especially those with a mismatched learning preference with the online learning culture, to be a better user of online education. Specifically, the instructors can set up a pre-course orientation module that covers generic guidance on learning how to learn in an online setting, communication on the awareness and respect for cross-cultural and intergenerational diversity, and specific descriptions of practical online learning strategies.

Information design is an often ignored, yet often effective online instructional technique. Specifically, a clear structure and an intuitive presentation of the online course content and activity items will enable adult learners to develop an overview of the semester-long learning flow and hence better plan their learning processes during the whole semester. It should also enable ease of navigation so that online learners will only use the least number of "clicks" to find the needed learning materials, tasks, and tools.

Blending Intrapersonal and Interpersonal Inquiries

In an online learning setting when the presence of the instructor becomes more indirect and less dominant, learners will play a more central and more self-regulated role in their learning processes. As observed, it is common for an online instructor to either design online learning as a correspondence-course-like, "content + support" process (Ke & Xie, 2009), or "put forth great efforts in grouping and pairing students" in different collaborative learning activities to honor the social view of learning (Ke & Carr-Chellman, 2006, p. 249). Our project findings imply that neither of the two instructional practices fully addresses the needs of a diversity of interpersonal and intrapersonal learning orientations and preferences. Therefore, a desirable planning of online learning activities should consider a blending between intrapersonal and interpersonal inquiries. For example, the design of evaluation and learning tasks should emphasize or allow for both individual and team effort. The planning of the knowledge construction processes should provide opportunities for both solitary absorption (e.g., reading comprehension via a list of individual inquiry questions) and collaborative exploration (e.g., online discussions).

Toward an Inclusive Learning Culture

We believe that integrating multiple processes of learning, ways of interacting, and parts of the self are essential to effective teaching among integrated learners across cultures. Mestizo, Native, Hispano, and other minority and nontraditional students in this study were highly articulate in sharing their processes of learning and made many suggestions for faculty. It is our hope that faculty continue to innovate new techniques as they work with an increasingly diverse population of learners. By using a strengths-based approach to teaching and learning across cultures, faculty can garner a wide variety of ways of being, learning, knowing, and doing from both integrated and individuated cultures. This will allow student learners to benefit both from their own ways of learning and from others' ways of learning.

References

Anderson, T. (2003). Modes of interaction in distance education: Recent developments and research questions. In M. Moore (Ed.), *Handbook of distance education* (pp. 129–144). Mahwah: Lawrence Erlbaum.

Brayboy, B. M. J., & Maughan, E. (2009). Native American knowledges and the story of the bean. *Harvard Educational Review, 79*(1), 1–21.

Covarrubias, P. O., & Windchief, S. W. (2009). Silences in stewardship: Some American Indian college students' examples. *The Howard Journal of Communications, 20*(4), 333–352.

Guido-DiBrito, F., & Chávez, A. F. (2003). Understanding the ethnic self: Learning and teaching in a multicultural world. *Journal of Student Affairs, 7*, 11–21.

Ibarra, R. (2001). *Beyond affirmative action: Reframing the context of higher education*. Madison: University of Wisconsin.

Ke, F., & Carr-Chellman, A. (2006). Solitary learner in online collaborative learning: A disappointing experience? *Quarterly Review of Distance Education, 7*(3), 249–265.

Ke, F., & Xie, K. (2009). Toward deep learning for adult students in online courses. *The Internet and Higher Education, 12*(3–4), 136–145.

Rendón, L. I. (2009). *Sentipensante (sensing/thinking) pedagogy: Educating for wholeness, social justice and liberation*. Sterling: Stylus.

Shea, V. (1994). *Netiquette*. San Francisco: Albion Books.

Chapter 9
Concluding Thoughts

Nurturing Inclusive Learning Cultures for Learner Diversification

Our study findings underscore the changing face of students and the need for evolving web-based learning contexts – design, facilitation, access, opportunity, resources, ways of learning, and technology. Ethnicity- and age-related learner differences, as our study findings suggest, play a role in online learners' commitment toward, perception of, and participation in different modes of online interactions. They also mediate learners' awareness and adaptation toward the external interaction/learning contexts. On the other hand, ethnicity- and age-related learner differences are changeable, not necessarily group-normed, and usually intermingled with other dimensions of individual learner differences. As such, it is challenging and potentially unrealistic to perform online instruction and instructional design based on certain preset assumptions or categorization of ethnicity- and age-related learner profiles. Besides the danger of composing stereotyping and tokenism in representing culture- and age-related learner needs, the practice of categorizing learners and their preferences based on their ethnic and age groups will fail to capture the cultural change (or adaptation) and the emergent learning culture that an online learner may experience during a specific online course setting.

Therefore, we propose that the core of cross-cultural and intergenerational instruction and design is not just being adaptive but encompasses nurturing of an inclusive, learning-oriented, diversity-valuing culture within an online course and endorsing of such a culture by both instructors and students. Such an endorsement effort should be integrated as a culturally inclusive design of the online learning contexts before the start of learning/teaching, as well as the fluid adaptation during the actual online teaching and learning processes.

F. Ke and A.F. Chávez, *Web-Based Teaching and Learning across Culture and Age*,

DOI 10.1007/978-1-4614-0863-5_9,

Negotiation of Inclusive Learning Culture and Flexibility for Individual Adaptation

Consistent with the previous proposition on developing online learning communities to promote cultural inclusivity (McLoughlin, 2001), we propose that an inclusive learning culture could be codeveloped and negotiated among members of a learning-unit-based cultural group (i.e., an online learning community). In a best-case scenario, this would comprise guidelines for learning and interaction that allow for flexible adaptation for different ethnicity-, age-related, or other cultural subgroups. A newly developed and negotiated inclusive learning culture could embrace existing culture-related learning preferences of diverse learner subgroups by emphasizing a constructive, versatile learning climate – one that highlights *personal relevance*, *authentic learning*, *active learning*, *student autonomy*, and *cultural awareness* and *adaptation.*

Inclusive cultural constructs are situated in online learners' acting and thinking during interactions with learning content, peers, and the instructor. For example, there could be a negotiated understanding between the instructor and learners about the amount, process, and desirable quality of peer interactions. A participatory design process could involve diverse student representatives in deciding when one should interact with peers (e.g., scheduled or spontaneous, frequency), to fulfill what purposes (e.g., metacognitive regulation, cognitive assimilation or accommodation, or emotional support), using what tools (e.g., synchronous or asynchronous), and following what quality profile (e.g., that depicts desirable content and ways of expression). Members of the learning-unit-based cultural group could also share, explore, and negotiate a preferred *flow* in interacting with and processing content objects and completing various learning activities (e.g., information comprehension, absorption, practice, and transfer). What resources should be processed, following what kind of sequence (e.g., reading independently before processing lecture materials)? What learning tasks are foundational and what are secondary, in what activity structure, following what timeline, using what quality standards, and why? All these questions should be elucidated while allowing flexible and emergent adaptation for the members of the learning-oriented cultural group. Last but not least, an online instructor could consult other members of the learning-unit-based cultural group on the expectations and representation approaches for the social and teaching presence of the online instructor, which relate to but are not limited to the following questions: What kind of role will this instructor play in the learner community or cultural group (e.g., an expert, a facilitator, and a mentor)? How will the instructor deliver his/her teaching and social presence (e.g., via live facilitation, feedback, e-lecturing, or pre-developed narratives)? How will the instructor interact with the whole group and individual learners?

The inclusive culture should never be rigid. It should be fluid and nurtured adaptively by respecting and extending the disciplinary or content-related culture; the ethnicity-, age-related, or other preexisting cultural preferences; and other relevant individual learner characteristics. As such, the presence and profile of an inclusive learning culture would vary across specific online courses or programs and even vary across semesters within the same course due to different dynamics, learning processes, and needs associated with different learner communities. Yet all inclusive cultural protocols should share or endorse a core set of parameters including (a) embracing and valuing diversity, (b) promoting authentic and active learning, and (c) fostering cultural awareness and adaptation.

A Cautionary Note

There are some significant cautions for negotiating an inclusive learning culture among online learners across culture and age. **First**, here are realities of power and cultural practices that are important to consider. Negotiation and communication during conflict vary greatly across cultures. Individuals in some cultures will strive for harmony in communal or public settings and are unlikely to engage in direct negotiations especially if conflict is likely. Even direct questioning by an instructor will not draw out the opinions of certain individuals. Because other cultures, especially many Northern European Caucasian American individuals, are comfortable and often welcome opportunities to give input or even engage in negotiations, it is critical that instructors develop ways other than direct public questioning about needs and preferences within the learner group. Several options are helpful in an online learning context, including forming anonymous discussions where students can offer their needs and opinions without names attached, asking students to offer learner preferences via the use of models such as the Cultural Constructs of Teaching and Learning in Chap. 5. This less direct and in many ways more specific kind of technique allows an instructor to then diversify learning/teaching designs with student input that is influenced more by student needs and preferences than by negative power issues, conflict aversion, or cultural norms.

Second, it is helpful for online instructors to keep in mind that cultural and age identities of students influence learning context dynamics in both subtle and overt ways. Students from more dominant US cultures including males, some older students, and Northern European Caucasian cultures may be less aware or accepting of their own identity dominance in teaching and learning practice. Students who are comfortable with and have been academically successful with traditional modes of teaching and learning are most likely to feel discomfort with other learning processes. For some students, this discomfort or sense of privilege may serve as a catalyst for open resistance to new or different ways of teaching and learning (Rendón, 2009; Turner, 1999). Instructors can help alleviate these kinds of dynamics by offering reassurance about facing discomfort as part of many learning processes and pointing out benefits of learning to interact and develop skills helpful within a highly diverse societal and work context.

Third, cultural, age, and gender identities also influence ways that students respond to instructors. Alternatives suggested or offered by faculty who are older, male, and Northern European Caucasian are more likely to be accepted as legitimate and helpful by students across identities. Instructors with this identity profile are often seen by students across identities as having the most authority, expertise, and legitimacy in the academic arena. The farther an instructor is from this identity profile, the more likely students will resist teaching design and facilitation that differs from traditional practices (Rendón, 2009; Turner, 1999). This social dynamic makes it difficult for some faculty to engage in transformative efforts to enhance learning across identity differences. Yet in our study, faculty from minority and mixed race/ethnic cultures were most likely to have a balance of cultural norms in their teaching design and facilitation.

Each of us as instructors brings strengths to this transformation. Those of us from dominant groups may find it harder to see and understand our own underlying cultural manifestations in how we teach yet easier to gain acceptance from students for alternatives. Those of us from less dominant groups are likely to find it easier to see and understand our own underlying cultural norms and their manifestations in our teaching yet may experience greater resistance from students when we offer alternative forms of pedagogy and facilitation. Discussing learning goals and pointing out benefits of learning across cultural norms for future work and life are often enough to alleviate resistance among students. Over time as well, students often relay their positive experiences in courses that are more culturally balanced in pedagogy and facilitation resulting in resistance diminishing over time.

Participatory and Deliberative Approaches

The development or nurturing of an inclusive learning culture within an online course or program can be achieved through a naturalistic, participatory approach and/or a preplanned, deliberative approach. The former focuses on involving all members (including both instructor and students) in negotiating and collaboratively deciding on norms and protocols for the three modes of learning interactions. As such, the development of learning/interaction materials and activities is usually fluid and consistently occurring through the school semester. The latter focuses on a conscious, deliberative design effort of the instructor or designer before the web-based teaching and learning process. For example, an instructor or designer, via learning content and activity design, materials development, and technology selection, can purposefully design multiple representations or options of learner-content, learner-learner, and learner-instructor interaction. The multiplicity in the interaction activity, material, and tool design will enable the later refining or adaptation through the school semester to address observed or reported learner diversification. Over time as well, instructors can incorporate student formal and informal feedback and requests into the overall design. Participatory and deliberative approaches can be viewed as two ends of a continuum and should be integrated and balanced dynamically.

One caution is learners differ in developmentally matureness from dualistic (right/wrong, good/bad) thinking processes toward a more relativistic orientation (there is some good and some bad in most things) (Evans, Forney, Guido, & Patton, 2009). This means that some students are more developmentally "ready" to engage in negotiations and to see the instructor as a facilitator of learning. Others may be locked firmly in a perspective that defines an instructor as the expert and students as those who only take in knowledge. Asking some students to create or critique knowledge and to learn from peers is something that younger (and sometimes older) students must grow into. This is also informed by cultural norms of education, teaching, and learning. Since some cultures define teaching and learning in collaborative, facilitative ways and others as one-way, top-down, individual students are likely to respond accordingly to being asked by instructors to engage in negotiations, collective design, and decision processes. Once again, offering rationales for moving in new directions, supporting students as both learners and teacher facilitators, and promoting learner knowledge as valid are all helpful to engaging students in collaborative design processes.

Cultural Awareness and Adaptation Fostering: Cultural, Teaching, and Learning Biographies Exploration

As part of purposeful training or orientation, both online instructors and students should be encouraged to explore and share their autobiographies in terms of culture-related preferences, teaching or learning philosophies, and the related design, teaching, or learning patterns. Our study findings suggest that most online instructors welcome either formal training or informal guidance about inclusive web-based teaching and instructional design. Online learners have indicated a sense of stress or frustration on cross-cultural adaptation. To promote cultural awareness and cross-cultural adaptation, culture-related teaching and learning biography writing and sharing would be helpful as a core element of professional development workshops or orientation sessions for online instructors and students. In addition, the competence of being culturally aware and adaptive should be counted as an explicit evaluation dimension or element for the instructor, course, and learner evaluation.

Such a cultural analysis and exploration should also be integrated into the general instructional development model (e.g., ADDIE) and the training of instructional designers to reinforce cultural awareness and adaptation. Several scholars have discussed or proposed the inclusion of cultural adaptation as an important, additional component in the existing online instructional design framework. As these scholars argued and our project findings confirmed, cultural adaption can act as an expansion of the needs and learner analysis phase by involving cultural analysis and culture knowledge experts during the learner and instructional context analysis (Edmundson, 2007; Rogers, Graham, & Mayers, 2007). Cultural adaptation can work as an explicit design goal to guide the participatory design process during the online learning environment design (e.g., Gunawardena, Wilson, & Nolla, 2003). Cultural adaption should also work as an evaluation criterion that should be appraised and considered throughout the instructional development, implementation, management, and evaluation phases (Parrish & Linder-VanBerschot, 2010; Young, 2008). Therefore, the programs of instructional design education should consider the provision of the training on culture-related instructional design models to prepare designers who are competent in inclusive learning environment design.

Some empirical work, led by one of the authors, is currently underway with two faculty cohorts at two universities around long-term development in the area of culture and college teaching/learning. As part of this process, faculty were each asked to write an autobiographical essay on how their own cultural assumptions, values, beliefs, and norms manifest in their teaching and in the way they interpret and interact with students. Over time, faculty were guided in processes to identify cultural origins and norms even when there was little or no cultural self-awareness for an individual faculty member. Though essays were privately held between faculty and facilitators, faculty were encouraged to share insights with other faculty in communal meetings over time, facilitated in culturally analyzing course syllabi, teaching practices, pedagogical design, and course materials in relation to their own cultural norms as well as in consideration of a diversity of student cultural norms. This introspective work has already served as a key aspect in the development of faculty capacity for teaching effectively across cultures in many disciplines and in many formats (online, face-to-face, studio, clinical, etc.). Research is underway to explore outcomes, insights, and experiences from this process.

Future Research

Our hope is that the study reported in this book serves as a catalyst for increased research on inclusive online instructional design and culture to promote deep learning for online students across culture and age. In this in situ study, the phenomenon of culture-related web-based teaching and learning is examined in its natural setting. We recommend that future investigation of web-based teaching and learning across culture and age adopt an experimental and design-based research approach that encompasses a series of design experiments to build on longitudinal evidence of interaction effects between online learning contexts reflecting inclusive learning culture, online learners' cultural and age-related characteristics, their learning and participation patterns, and learning outcomes.

In addition, this current study focuses on examining learners' performance of different modes of learning interactions, learning participation processes, and self-perceived learning success and satisfaction as major measures of learner success. A future study on the inclusive web-based teaching and learning would benefit from other measures of online learning success, such as the quality of assignment/project completion and other summative measures on learning objectives achievement.

In our project, we focused on examining ethnic and age-related learner diversity. Because of the confined nature of our cases and sampling site, study findings should be taken with caution when transferred to other cultural groups or educational settings. Future research would benefit from cross-site comparison and additional nationality and ethnicity-related cultural groups (e.g., African American, Asian and Pacific Islander, International, Middle Eastern American, Jewish American) to examine whether similar findings are replicated.

Implications for Higher Education

There are numerous implications for higher education that arise from rapidly developing web-based learning especially across culture and age. One of the great challenges of this new era of colleges and universities is the sheer amount of foundational change required to keep up in this evolving educational world. These include evolving institutional structures, policy, finance, and academic forms; emerging technologies; widening access; new definitions of student life; and changing faculty and staff roles. The following sections offer some glimpses into these areas of change in higher education.

Evolving Institutional Models

The advent of web-based collegiate learning contexts may be the most influential catalyst for institutional change since the GI Bill and other forms of financial aid. In addition to change in current institutions, new collegiate institutions are cropping up in every shape and form especially in proprietary guise to take advantage of new technologies and lure students into their edu-business models. Many students of color are first generation college learners and are likely to be less knowledgeable about college and likely to be more susceptible to advertising for less than reputable institutions. Because students of color are also often more savvy about discrimination and difference, institutions of higher education are most likely to experience success in recruitment when offering an open and candid discussion to prospective students about the benefits and limitations of enrolling in their institution. This is often interpreted by students of color regardless of socioeconomic class or family history with college attendance, as a show of care for student needs and fit rather than institutional benefit.

States and higher education institutions struggle to craft funding models and develop policy effective in this web-based learning context. Colleges and universities use varying forms of incentives including alternate pay models, mandatory assignments to encourage or require faculty to participate. Embedding student retention and learning into tenure models for all modes of teaching is a largely missing and much needed addition to policy. When faculty are rewarded through the job security of tenure, as well as promotion and merit pay for tenured, tenure track, and adjunct faculty, individual instructors are more likely to engage in necessary professional development and effective teaching practices.

Training for online teaching as well as technical support and design requires new and complex structures and finance as well as ongoing and significant time from faculty. Because identities such as culture and age are complex and have deep influence on both teaching and learning, professional development is most beneficial when ongoing, cohort based, and in-depth. Introspective and outward looking professional development is needed for faculty to learn how their own identities manifest in teaching as well as how student identities manifest in learning.

Academic policy is evolving as the realities of teaching and learning in cyberspace create new challenges for accountability with plagiarism, evaluation, and testing, as well as other forms of cheating. Finding ways to assist faculty in design as well as accountability within teaching and learning contexts will continue to evolve with collegiate institutions, changing student demographics, and evolving technologies.

Widening and Differentiating Access

Unprecedented numbers of new student populations are enrolling through this new form of access to a college degree including students who work full time, older students, students with children, students from underrepresented ethnic/racial/cultural populations, students in rural areas, and international students who are remaining in their home countries. Individuals find they can maintain extended family and cultural ties, live where they choose, and maintain work lives while obtaining a college degree or needed classes for professional development or personal enrichment. Some populations such as Native Americans living in remote communities have embraced online education as a form of college that enables upholding familial, cultural, spiritual, and tribal responsibilities and ties. Many, however, face access challenges that can often be alleviated through college-community partnerships such as the Internet to the Hogan program (www.navajotech.edu/index.php/ith) sponsored by the Navajo Nation, several tribal colleges, National Science Foundation, and the university in a multistate area.

As with any financially or physically reliant activity, differential access is evident. Low-income students have lesser financial ability to obtain technologies and Internet access necessary for web-based learning though many communities work hard to provide access and equipment especially through schools, community centers, and libraries. Rural students face access issues both in constant and intermittent realities, often negotiating web connections that come in and out or no access at all. As always, low-income and rural students face additional challenges to gaining a college degree.

New Forms of Student Life

The face of student life is rapidly changing from the traditional college experience of living and working on campus, attending classes, and experiencing college together with peers. Many students now combine some campus-based courses with those offered online, interacting with other students mostly in class, via study groups, and during quick meals when they are on campus. Many others juggle full-time jobs, choose colleges that offer fully online degrees in their chosen fields, and consider professional peers and their own families as their focus outside of college and do not consider campus life a part of their reality. Advising, interactions with instructors, and other necessary collegiate services take on a whole new meaning as some students never come to campus. Within some institutions, students are able to do everything online from admissions to graduation. Some may lament the decline of student life on campuses, yet even the most skeptical acknowledge that web-based collegiate education is here to stay.

Emerging Technologies

Rapidly emerging technological hardware and software make web-based teaching and learning a constant opportunity and challenge for all involved. Students must add this to their list of things to learn and negotiate often during the middle of a degree or course. Faculty must respond to ever changing web-based teaching systems, reliance on often overtaxed technological support professionals, and what to do when technologies fail during instruction. Conversely, students and faculty benefit from "all the marvelous possibilities" of endlessly developing technologies and online resources and knowledge bases.

Changing Faculty and Staff Roles

Professional roles on campus are changing as increasing numbers of students choose or demand web-based forms of instruction. In some departments, face-to-face courses go unfilled while waiting lists abound for online courses. In others, faculty and/or students continue to choose classroom-based learning or fully online degrees. Effective teaching online can take upwards of three times the amount of time to teach than the equivalent face-to-face time because of additional design, technology requirements, as well as student expectations for continual responsiveness and access of instructors. Some students now resist or completely shun attending campus office hours to interact with instructors, preferring instead to ask questions via e-mail, online office hours, or by phone or Skype. Meetings are rapidly becoming a hybrid of professionals who are physically present combined with those who are in attendance via the Internet or phone conferencing. Staff infrastructures are also required as new forms of expertise and support are called for to support web-based forms of learning, communications, services, and interactions.

There is a definite generational and technological gap between many students who are technological insiders or naturalized almost from birth into not only multiple technologies but also multiple social networks and Internet resources and faculty who are usually technological outsiders, foreigners, or immigrants at best. This will change over time as more and more faculty are hired who have grown up within this new technological world.

In conclusion, colleges and universities as well as the faculty, staff, and students in these communities face many opportunities and challenges because of this rapidly evolving reality in the context of teaching and learning. There are many exciting and challenging times ahead.

References

Edmundson, A. (Ed.). (2007). *Globalized e-learning cultural challenges*. Hershey: Information Science Publishing.

Evans, N. J., Forney, D. S., & Guido-DiBrito, F. (2009). *Student development in college: Theory, research and practice*. San Francisco: Jossey-Bass.

Gunawardena, C., Wilson, P., & Nolla, A. (2003). Culture and online education. In M. Morre & W. Anderson (Eds.), *Handbook of distance education* (pp. 753–775). Mahwah: Lawrence Erlbaum.

McLoughlin, C. (2001). Inclusivity and alignment: Principles of pedagogy, task and assessment design for effective cross-cultural online learning. *Distance Education, 22*(1), 7–29.

Parrish, P., & Linder-VanBerschot, J. A. (2010). Cultural dimensions of learning: Addressing the challenges of multicultural instruction. *International Review of Research in Open and Distance Learning, 11*(2), 1–19.

Rendón, L. I. (2009). *Sentipensante (sensing/thinking) pedagogy: Educating for wholeness, social justice and liberation*. Sterling: Stylus.

Rogers, P. C., Graham, C. R., & Mayes, C. T. (2007). Cultural competence and instructional design: Exploration research into the delivery of online instruction cross-culturally. *Educational Technology Research and Development, 55*(2), 197–217.

Turner, C. S. (1999). *Faculty of color in academe: Bittersweet success*. Upper Saddle River: Pearson Education Publishers.

Young, P. A. (2008). The culture based model: Constructing a model of culture. *Educational Technology & Society, 11*(2), 107–118.

Index

F. Ke and A.F. Chávez, *Web-Based Teaching and Learning across Culture and Age*,
DOI 10.1007/978-1-4614-0863-5,

9781461408628